IDEAS FOR USING THESE WORKSHEE

- As **CLASSWORK SHEETS,** which can be mad … on with the revision guide.
- As **HOMEWORK SHEETS,** with differentiate… …ities.
- As a **STRUCTURED REVISION PROGRAMME** in the months preceding the National Curriculum Tests.
- As **TEST MATERIAL** to test understanding of individual or groups of topics.

and last but not least . . .

- As an **EMERGENCY MEASURE** for when staff are absent at short notice.

A NOTE TO TEACHERS AND PARENTS ...

Because the National Curriculum Test material tends to be relatively lightweight in terms of the demands made on the children to write, we have deliberately compromised in order to provide 15 minute worksheets which reinforce classroom learning as well as providing experience of test material. These worksheets have been designed to be very easy to mark but we suggest that pupils use pencils so that corrections can be done neatly. All the Worksheets are cross-referenced to the best-selling revision guide "THE ESSENTIALS OF SCIENCE: KEY STAGE TWO" by Grace A. Adams.

A NOTE TO THE PUPIL ...

We hope that you will enjoy working through this book and that you will use a pencil to answer the questions in the spaces provided. These spaces are indicated by a ✎ symbol. If you have a copy of the revision guide: "THE ESSENTIALS OF SCIENCE: KEY STAGE TWO" by Grace A. Adams, you can use it to help you as the pages in each book match each other.

Good Luck!!

NATIONAL CURRICULUM 2000

These Pupil Worksheets have been fully revised and updated to comply with the changes made to the National Curriculum Programme of Study.

All these worksheets are cross-referenced to the best-selling revision guide
"THE ESSENTIALS OF SCIENCE: KEY STAGE TWO" by Grace A. Adams.

LIVING AND NON - LIVING THINGS

1. Andrew and Dianne went for a walk in the woods to look at different animals. Which things do ALL animals do?

Tick the boxes below if you think all animals do these things:

Swim ☐	Make sounds ☐	Eat ☐
Grow ☐	Reproduce ☐	Move ☐
See ☐	Sense things ☐	Hunt ☐
Kill things ☐	Hide at night ☐	Listen ☐

2. a) Which of our senses do we use when we do the following things (careful! there may be more than one):

Enjoying our school dinner ______

Reading a book ______

Stroking a pet animal ______

Listening to music ______

b) Say which of your senses you would least like to lose. Explain your reasons.

______

______

______

3. Fill in the following crossword with 5 life processes which all animals show.

When you have put the words in, write clues for each one in the spaces below:

1. DOWN ______

______

2. & 3. DOWN ______

______

4. ACROSS ______

______

5. ACROSS ______

6. ACROSS ______

1. a) Why do animals, including humans, have teeth?

b) This type of tooth is called an INCISOR.

Explain how it is well designed for the job it does.

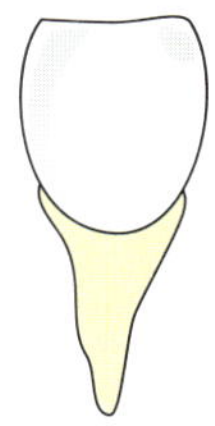

c) This type of tooth is called a MOLAR.

Explain how it is well designed for the job it does.

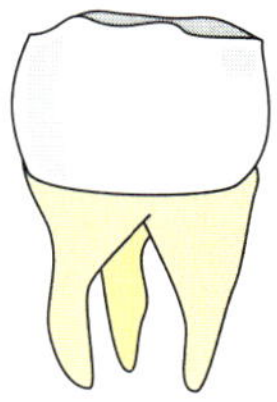

2. The diagrams show the skulls and teeth of a sheep, and a dog.

A SHEEP'S SKULL AND TEETH

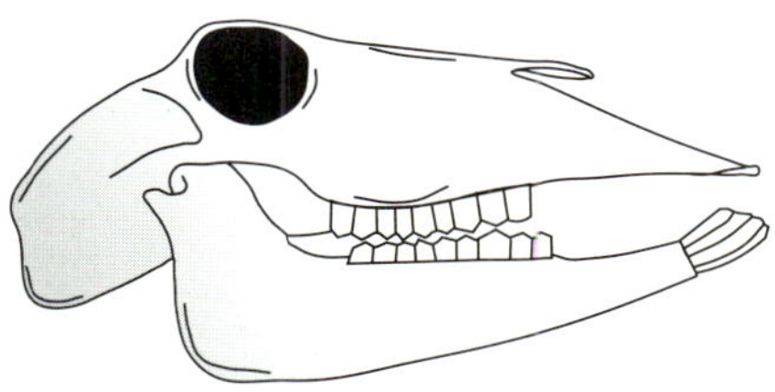

A DOG'S SKULL AND TEETH

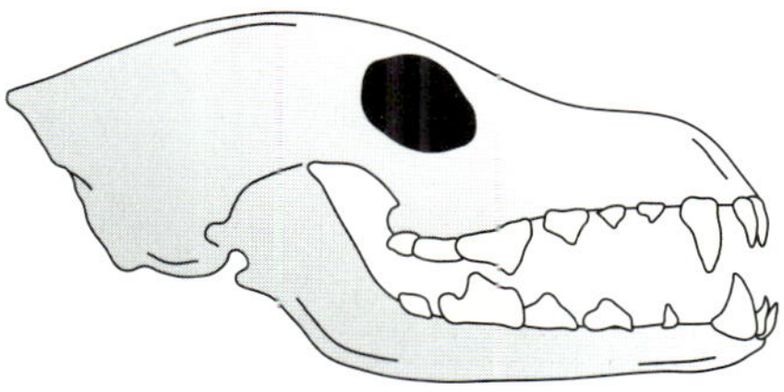

Explain the differences between the teeth of these animals. Remember that sheep eat mainly grass.

3. Make up a short poem about cleaning your teeth. Imagine that the poem is going to appear on a T.V. advert to encourage children to brush their teeth.

FOOD TYPES AND DIET

1. a) Make a list of 5 types of food which help growth.

   b) Make a list of 5 types of food which help us to be active.

   c) Make a list of 3 types of food which contain a lot of fat.

   d) Make a list of 3 types of food which contain a lot of sugar.

2. From the foods opposite:

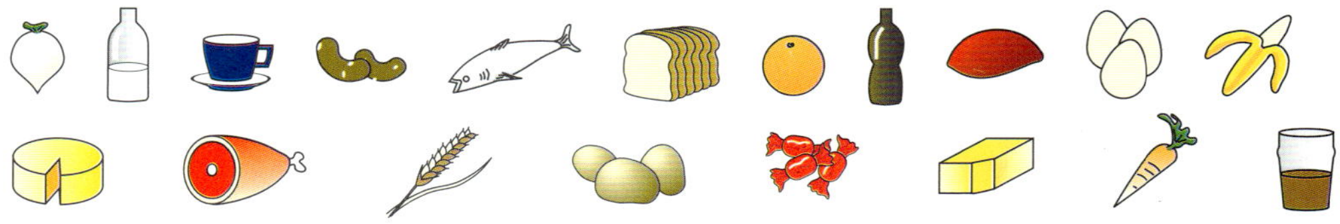

   a) Pick out those foods which contain quite a lot of starch.

   b) Pick out those foods which have come from animals.

   c) Pick out those foods which contain the most fat.

3. a) It is important not to eat too much sugary food. Why is this?

   b) It is important not to eat too much fatty food. Explain what might happen to you if you often ate lots of fatty food.

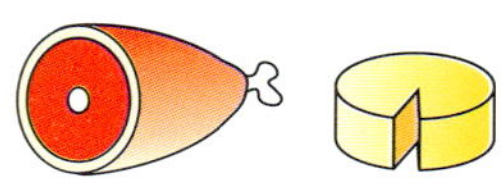

   c) Try to write a 'catchy' slogan for an advertisement to encourage people to eat healthily.

CIRCULATORY SYSTEM

1. Use the words in the boxes to fill in the gaps in the sentences below.

BODY	OXYGEN	BLOOD VESSELS	NO OXYGEN	LUNGS	AWAY FROM	TOWARDS

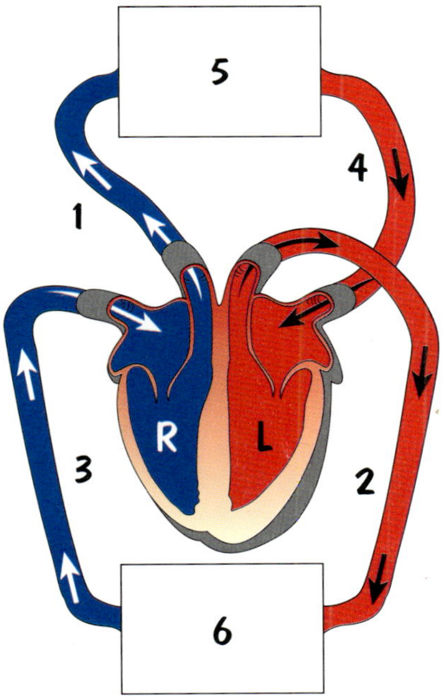

a) The structures labelled 1 and 2 are called ______

They carry blood ______ the heart.

b) The structures labelled 3 and 4 carry blood ______ the heart.

c) Blood going into, and leaving the left side of the heart has ______ in it.

d) Blood returning to, and leaving the right side of the heart has ______ in it.

e) Structure 5 is the ______

f) Structure 6 is the ______

2. Imagine you were in a tiny submarine travelling through the circulatory system. Place these signposts in the correct order in which you would pass them - starting with the lungs. Tick each sign as you use it!

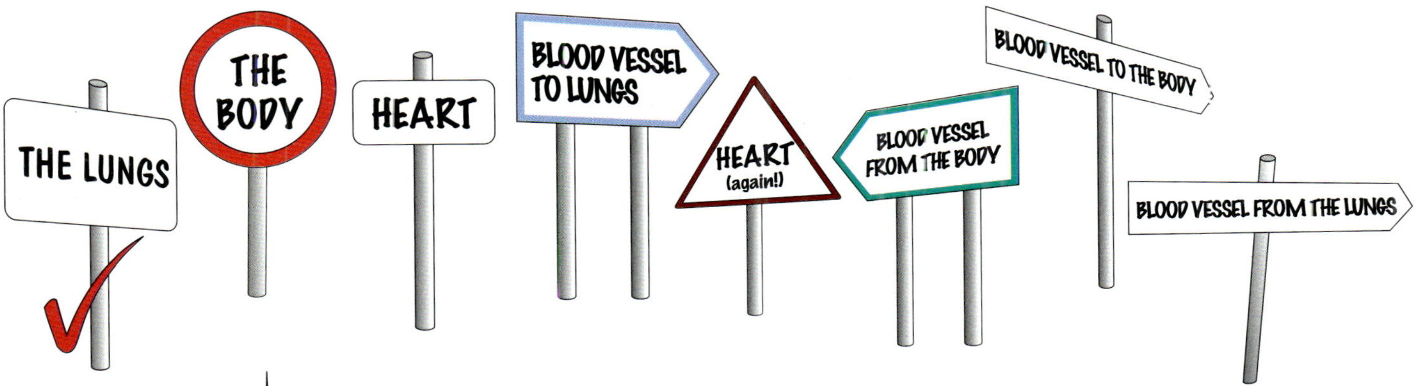

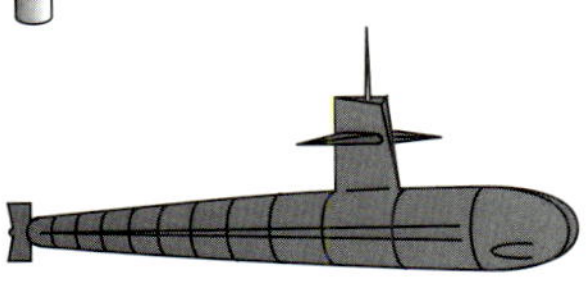

1. THE LUNGS → 2. ______ → 3. ______ → 4. ______

5. ______ → 6. ______ → 7. ______ → 8. ______

HEALTHY HEART AND PULSE RATE

1. Simon is 18 years old. He loves 'fast' food such as Hamburgers, Pizzas, Kebabs and Fish & Chips. He also loves drinking fizzy drinks such as Cola and Lemonade. Simon also smokes 20 cigarettes a day and even a short run for the bus leaves him panting for breath. He takes very little exercise because he prefers to sit in front of the T.V. in the evening.

a) List three things which are wrong with Simon's lifestyle.

b) Suggest three things he could do to start leading a much healthier life.

2. Jameel and James did press-ups for a full minute as hard as they could. They then stopped, sat down, and measured their PULSE RATES every two minutes. They got these results ...

Name	Pulse after exercise	Pulse after 2 mins	Pulse after 4 mins	Pulse after 6 mins	Pulse after 8 mins	Pulse after 10 mins
Jameel	164	124	106	94	84	78
James	168	136	118	104	96	88

a) Plot these results onto the graph opposite.

b) Try doing this yourself and plot your own results on the graph in a different colour.

3. Who do you think is the fitter of the two boys? Explain your answer.

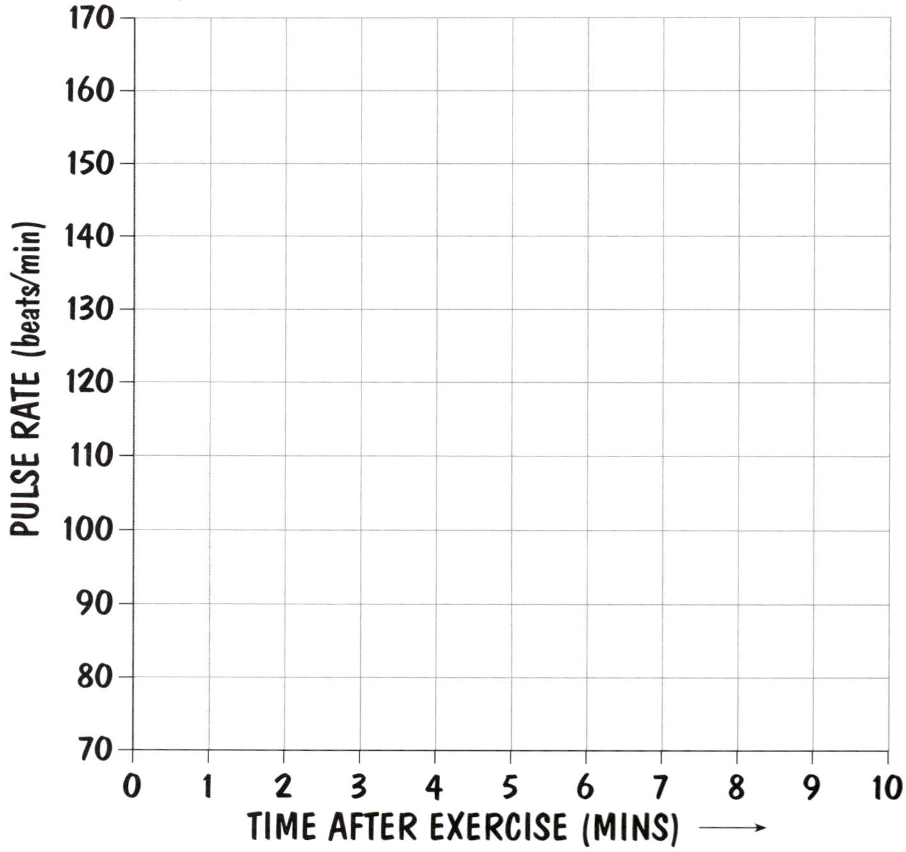

1. Here are some outlines of the bodies of different living things.

Draw in where you think the bones of the skeleton would be. One has been done for you (just think where they would need to be!!).

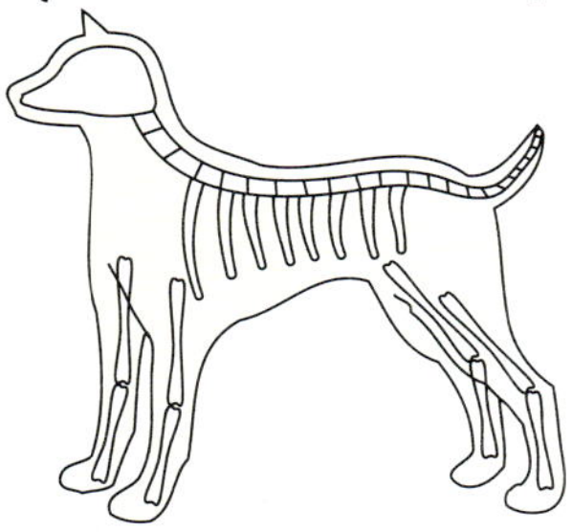

DOG

FISH

RABBIT

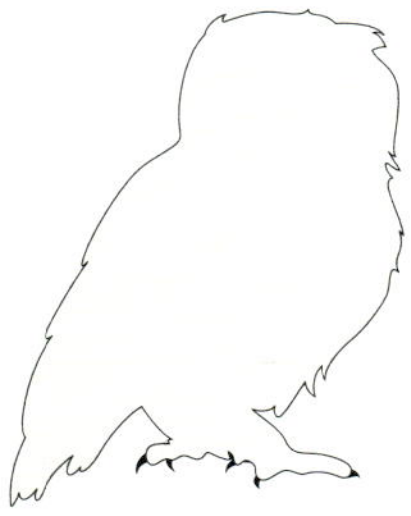

OWL

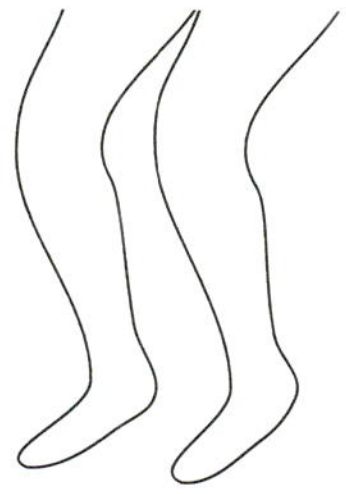

HUMAN LEGS

LAMB

2. Look at the diagrams below of an arm and a leg.

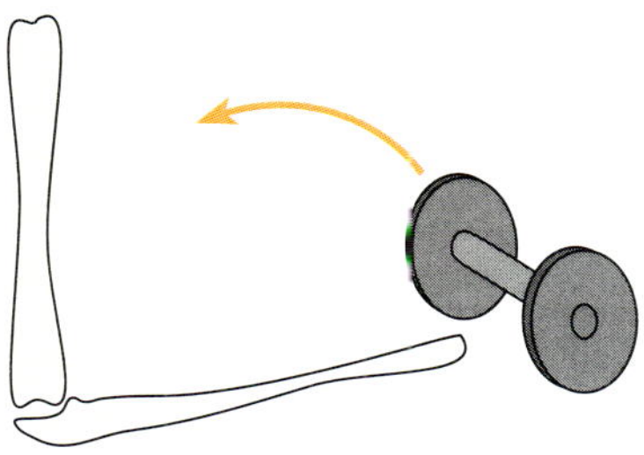

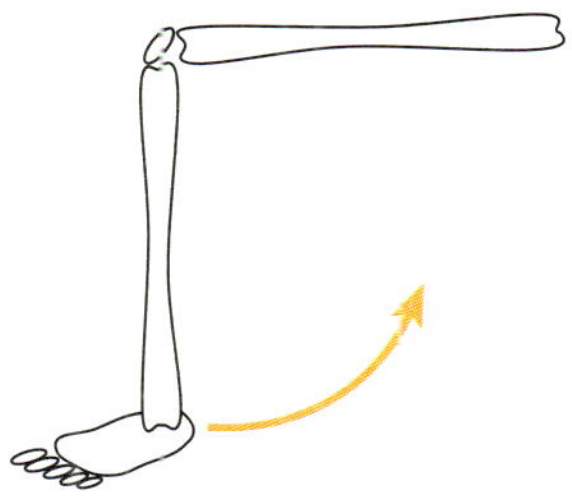

a) Draw in a muscle which would have to CONTRACT to move the weight in the direction shown.

b) Draw in a muscle which would have to RELAX to allow the leg to move in the direction shown.

3. a) Write a few lines describing how the skeleton could protect you if you were involved in a car accident.

____

____

____

b) Where do you think the strongest muscles are in your body? Explain your answer.

____

____

____

1. Describe the main features of each of these stages in the human life cycle.

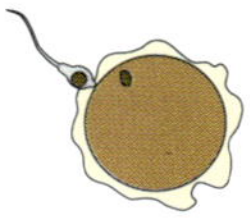
FERTILISATION

BIRTH

GROWTH

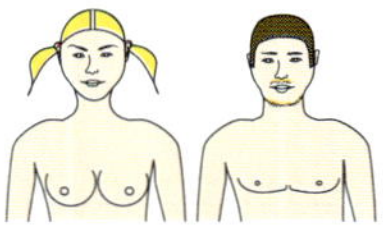
ADOLESCENCE

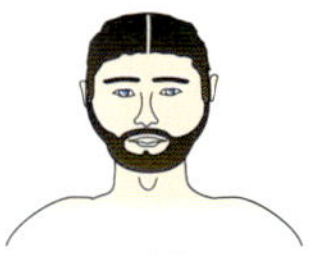
ADULTHOOD

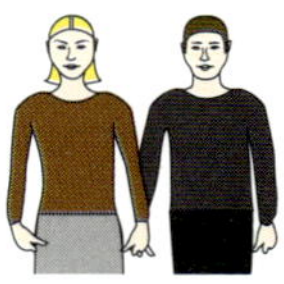
COURTSHIP

2. Draw some simple diagrams to show the life cycle of a butterfly.

3. Write down the main stages in the life cycle of a frog.

1. There are 10 words hidden in the word search below. They are all problems which can be caused by smoking. See if you can find them and write them in the space provided.

K	J	H	G	F	E	V	A	W	X	Y	Z	L	C	O	W	D	R	U	S
L	H	T	E	E	T	W	O	L	L	E	Y	D	A	T	E	L	L	T	T
M	N	S	H	C	D	B	A	B	A	U	O	I	O	I	S	O	I	E	R
O	P	Q	B	R	O	N	C	H	I	T	I	S	L	R	R	R	S	R	I
R	S	H	T	U	O	M	E	F	E	G	A	E	U	O	I	E	T	M	N
T	U	R	E	C	N	A	C	O	U	I	E	A	N	N	N	L	T	I	G
E	S	A	E	S	I	D	T	R	A	E	H	S	G	T	K	I	O	R	O
I	O	U	B	C	D	E	F	C	I	N	F	E	C	T	I	O	N	S	A
G	S	H	T	A	E	R	B	D	A	B	T	O	A	T	U	B	E	O	L
T	V	V	I	E	L	O	P	U	S	N	W	E	N	R	H	O	L	N	I
W	E	E	A	G	N	I	H	G	U	O	C	A	C	I	O	I	O	D	O
E	C	R	T	E	L	E	P	H	I	S	T	E	E	S	R	Z	N	E	N
T	T	V	W	E	S	T	T	O	W	L	E	R	R	T	R	Y	I	N	G

A ______

B ______

C ______

D ______

E ______

F ______

G ______

H ______

I ______

2. a) Manisha is a keen tennis player. She also smokes 10 cigarettes a day. Explain how smoking may affect Manisha when she is on the tennis court.

______

______

______

b) Some of Manisha's friends complain that her smoking also affects them. Explain how this could happen and what it might do to them.

______

______

c) Some of Manisha's friends also drink small amounts of alcohol (they are over 18). If they drink too much, which two organs in their bodies may be damaged?

______

3. Look at the list below. Put a circle around all the things which you can catch from other people. To check your answer, do the multiplication alongside it. If the answer is an EVEN number you can't catch it from other people. If the answer is an ODD number you can catch it!

TOOTHACHE 21 x 6	BALDNESS 32 x 8	CHICKEN POX 17 x 5	BROKEN LEG 14 x 12
MEASLES 19 x 7	ASTHMA 9 x 8	FLU 11 x 9	ECZEMA 10 x 18
COLDS 23 x 13	BRONCHITIS 14 x 8	CANCER 8 x 12	HEART DISEASE 24 x 16
MUMPS 13 x 13			

1. Olivia did an experiment to see if light was necessary for grass to grow well. She took a piece of black polythene sheet measuring 1m x 1m and pegged it out over an area of the school playing field.

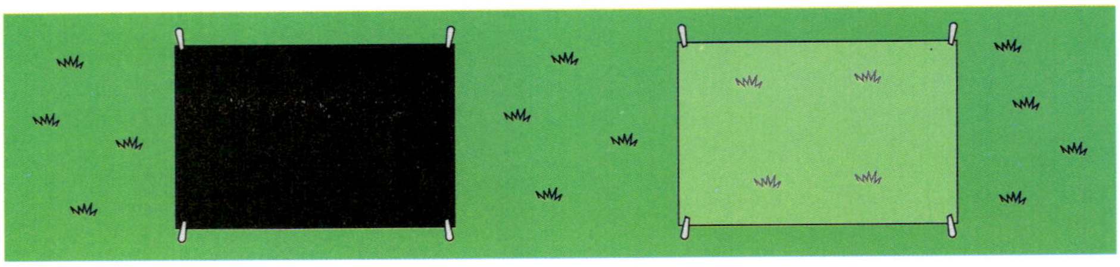

Quite close to it, she also pegged out a 1m x 1m piece of CLEAR polythene sheet. After a week she removed both sheets.

AFTER ONE WEEK...

a) What has happened to the grass which was covered by the black sheet?

b) Why did Olivia put a clear sheet down as well as a black one?

c) What conclusion can you come up with to explain these results?

2. Irfan noticed that moss (a very simple plant) grows on one side of the statue in the town square but not on the other side. He also noticed that there was more moss near the base of the statue.
How could he explain this?

3. Imagine you were doing an experiment to investigate the effect of temperature on how quickly cress seedlings grow. Make a list of all the things that you would need to keep the <u>same</u> in order to make it a FAIR TEST!

1. Fill in the boxes with the name of the part of the plant which is indicated.

A

B

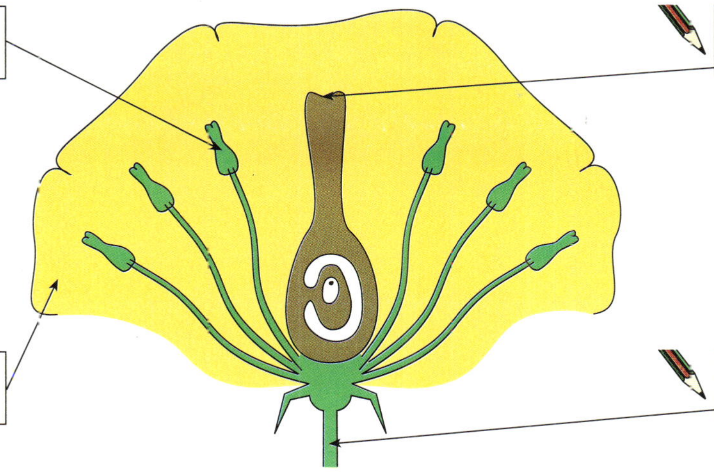

C

D

2. Draw a line connecting the part of the plant to the correct description.

STIGMA	Male part of the plant. Produces pollen.
STAMEN	Supports the leaves and flowers. Transports water.
OVARY	Part of the Carpel. Receives pollen from other plants.
PETALS	Contains egg cells.
STEM	Brightly coloured to attract insects.

3. a) Which part of the plant produces new material ('food') for growth?

b) Which three things are needed by the plant in order to produce food?

(i) (ii) (iii)

4. Michael did an investigation in which he grew cress seedlings in rich peaty soil and others in sand. After a week he took them out to measure the length of the roots. The diagram shows what he found. Explain his results.

'peaty' soil 'sandy' soil

LIFE CYCLE OF FLOWERING PLANTS

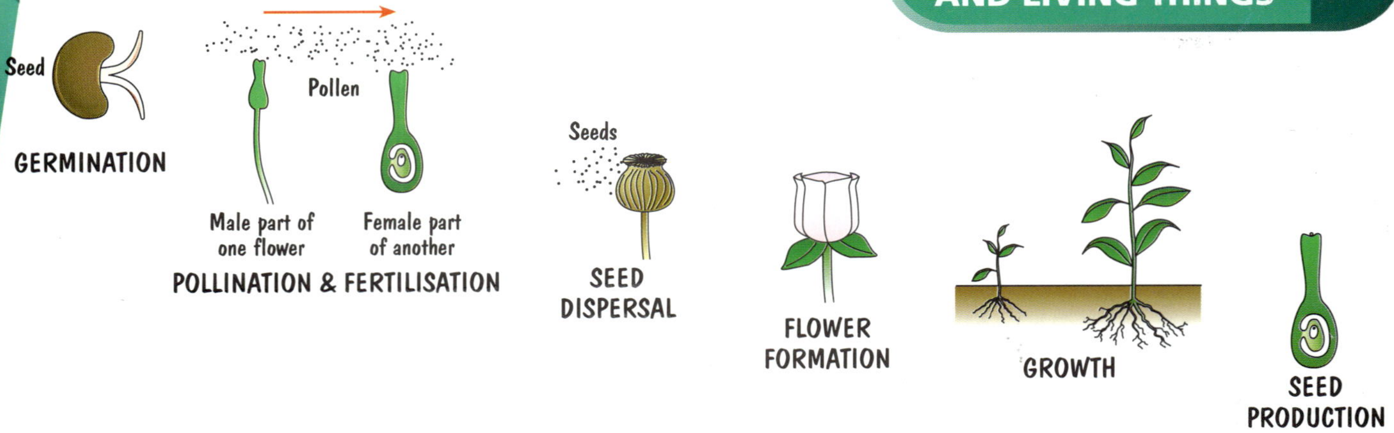

1. Rearrange these six stages of the life cycle of a flowering plant in the correct order in which they occur, starting with Germination...

GERMINATION					

2. John and Iestyn decided to investigate the growth of a weed from a seed they found in their garden. They measured it every 5 days and noted any changes to it. These were their results.

No of days	Length	Observations
0	0 cm	———
5	1 cm	Two small leaves
10	2 cm	———
15	4 cm	Two more leaves
20	6 cm	———
25	9 cm	Two more leaves
30	12 cm	A tiny flower
35	12 cm	———

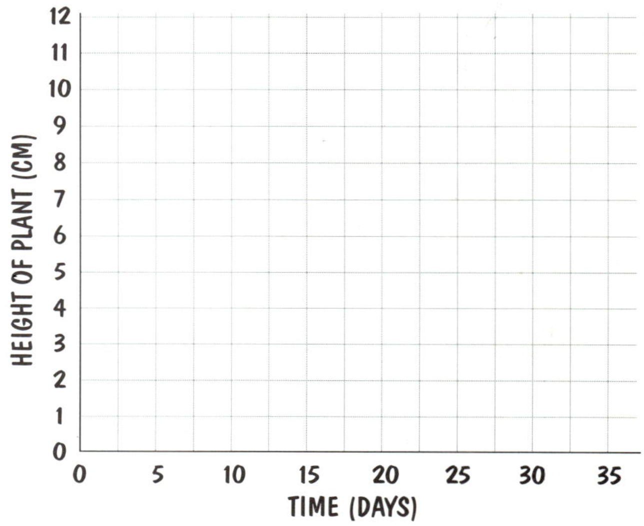

a) Plot these results on the graph opposite.

b) Mark on the graph in green crayon when the leaves appear, and in yellow crayon when the flower appears.

c) Why do you think the plant has stopped growing after 30 days?

3. Imagine you are a plant that is pollinated by insects.
Write down the things you would have which would be attractive to insects.

1. Joshua and Carol are investigating how well seeds are dispersed from two different plants.

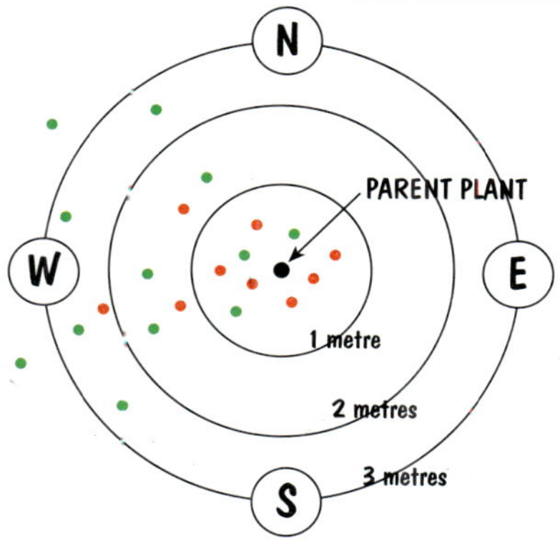

Both these plants disperse their seeds by gradually drying out and then springing open so their seeds are 'flicked away'. We call this dispersal by 'EXPLOSION'!
Joshua and Carol chose plants in different areas but decided to plot the positions of the seeds they found onto the same chart above. They marked the positions of the seeds in different colours.

a) From which direction was the wind blowing?

b) Estimate the furthest distance travelled by a Wallflower seed.

c) Estimate the furthest distance travelled by a Honesty seed.

d) Which plant is better at dispersing its seeds?

e) Name one thing that Joshua and Carol would have had to do in order to make this a FAIR TEST.

2. a) The Sycamore seed opposite would be likely to travel further than the seeds above. Why is this?

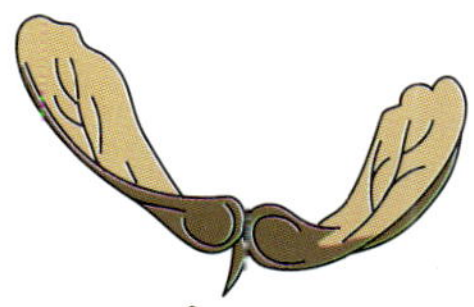
Sycamore

b) The Goosegrass seed would also be likely to travel further. Explain why this would happen.

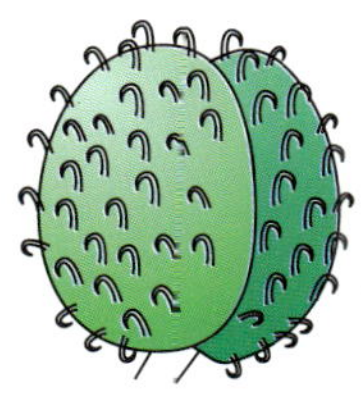
Cleavers (goosegrass)

3. Explain one other way in which seeds may be dispersed. Give an example if you can.

1. Use the key below to identify the animals labelled A-E.

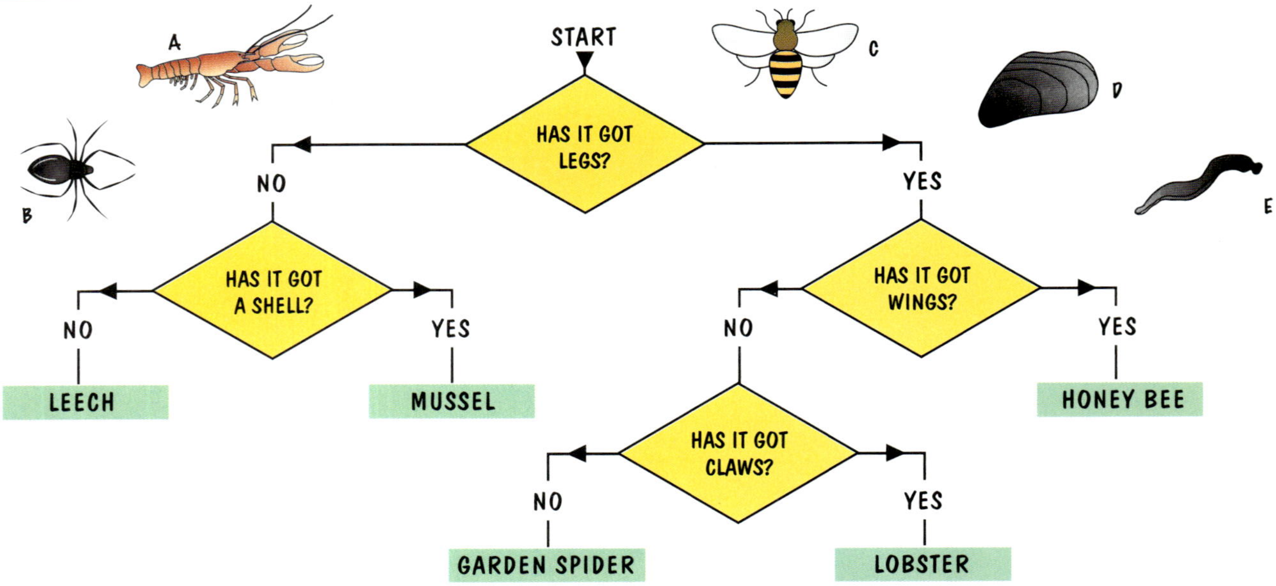

A	B	C	D	E

2. Use the key below to identify the animals labelled F-J.

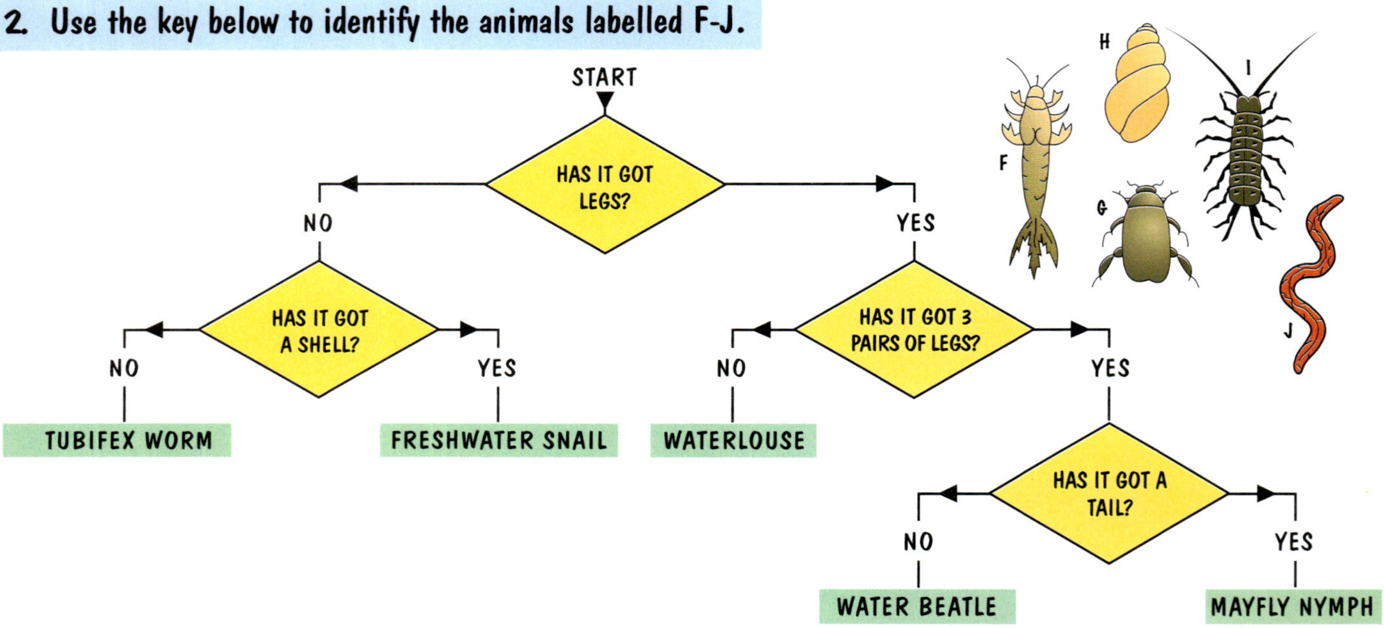

F	G	H	I	J

3. Make your own key in the space below to identify these 4 mammals.

SQUIRREL

BAT

DOLPHIN

OTTER

1. For each of the following animals, try to describe the environment in which you would commonly find it, and one way in which the animal is well suited to its environment.

Common Mussel

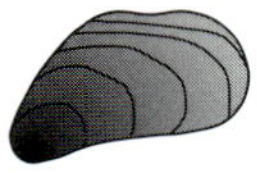

Common Earthworm

Garden Spider

Trout

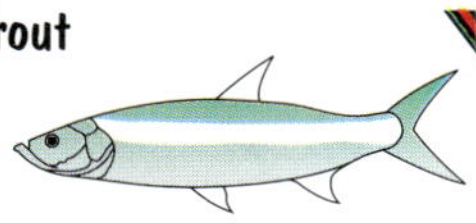

Barn Owl

Seal

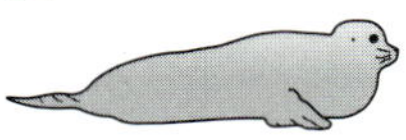

Rabbit

2. Now choose an animal yourself, and describe how it is well suited to its environment.

1. From all the different animals and plants shown above, try to make four food chains containing 3 living organisms, and three food chains containing 4 living organisms.

a) ______ → ______ → ______

b) ______ → ______ → ______

c) ______ → ______ → ______

d) ______ → ______ → ______

e) ______ → ______ → ______ → ______

f) ______ → ______ → ______ → ______

g) ______ → ______ → ______ → ______

2. Look at the food chain ...

Lettuce → Slug → Mistle Thrush → Hawk

a) What would happen to the number of Hawks in this food chain if all the slugs died?

______

b) What would happen to the number of mistle thrush if there was a bumper crop of lettuce?

______

1. Imagine you are trying to describe the following materials to someone who can't see them. You are not allowed to name the material but you can use as many descriptive words as you like.

Steel Fork 

Plastic Phone 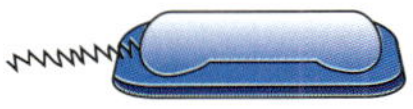

Glass Tumbler 

Rubber Eraser 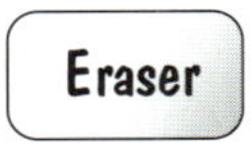

Woolly Jumper 

Elastic Band 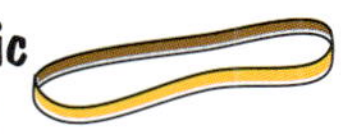

Fibreglass Fishing Rod 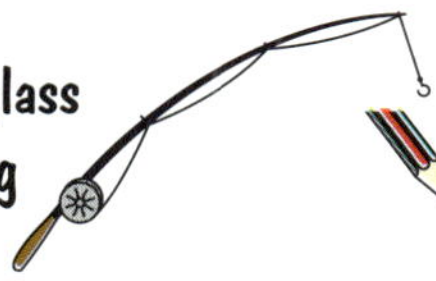

Stone Statue 

Leather Belt 

Copper Wire 

Here are some words you can use: Fibrous, bendy, springy, transparent, fluffy, brittle, attracted by a magnet, hairy, elastic, stretchy, light, flexible, opaque, natural material, tough, hard, strong, hard wearing, good electrical conductor.

1. Steven and Zoe were trying to sort out lots of different materials into groups, so that each group had materials with similar properties. See if you can help them to place these materials into the bins provided, and then think of a name to describe the materials in each bin. (use as many bins as you can!)

COTTON | STEEL KNIFE | LIGHT BULB | BRASS PAPERWEIGHT | WINE GLASS | STRING | THERMOMETER

PAPER TOWELS | TISSUES | PINS | CLOTH | NAILS | BROWN PAPER | ELECTRIC IRON | ALUMINIUM PAN

NEWSPAPER | MAGNIFYING GLASS | POP BOTTLE | EGG TIMER | SHIRT | BIRO | CREDIT CARD

GLASS MARBLE | NYLON BLOUSE | PENCIL SHARPENER | SHIRT BUTTON | MIRROR | RULER

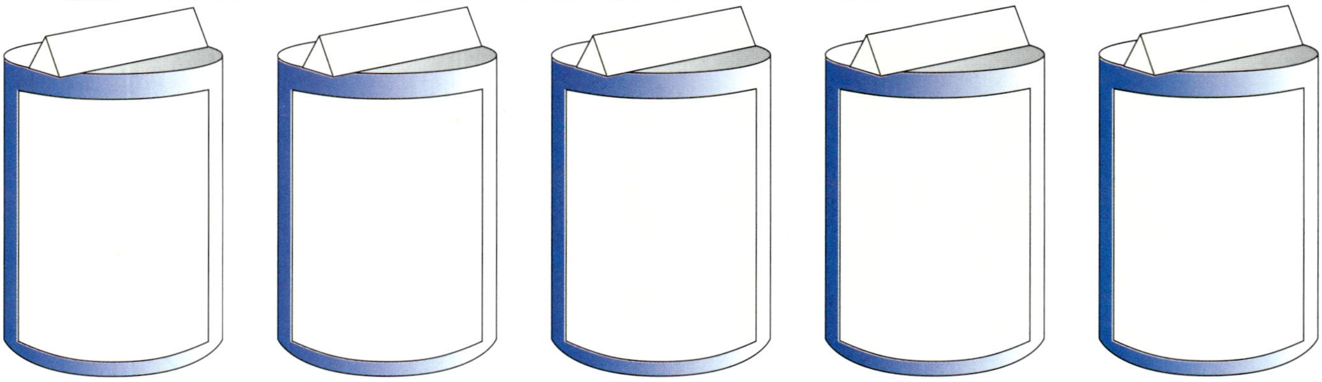

2. Steven and Zoe then decided to see which type of paper towel was best at mopping up water. They cut squares from each of the different types and weighed them. They then dipped them into the water, shook them gently, and weighed them again to see how much water they were holding. Here are their results ...

KLEENO	MOPPO	ABSORBO
gained 3 grams	gained 4 grams	gained 5 grams

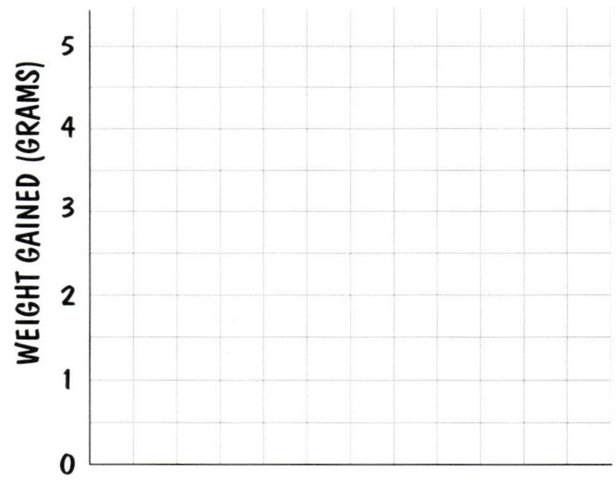

a) Draw a bar chart to show these results.

b) Which of the three paper towels was the most absorbent (best at mopping up!)

c) What would Steven and Zoe have had to keep the same to make this a FAIR TEST?

3. You can investigate the stretchiness of different types of elastic band quite simply in the classroom by hanging a weight from each band. If you were to do this for 4 different bands, ...

a) Describe what you would measure

b) Describe what you would keep the same to make it a FAIR TEST.

1. A material which is a good thermal insulator is one which prevents the transfer of heat across it. Explain how we use such materials in order to achieve the following ...

a) Keeping warm when we go outside on a cold winter's day.

b) Keeping our hot water supply as hot as possible without spending too much money on heating bills. (Think of the tank upstairs!)

c) Keeping the tea hot in the tea pot.

d) Keeping your dog warm in its basket.

e) Keeping ourselves warm in bed.

2. What do all the materials in your answers above have in common.

3. Kiran and Mark are investigating thermal conduction in three materials, copper, iron and glass. They set up their equipment as in the diagram opposite, and timed how long it took for the heat to travel along the rods and melt the wax holding the drawing pins.

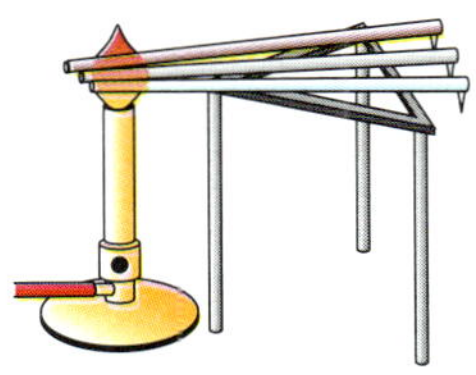

Here are their results ...
Glass rod 7 mins 20 secs, Copper rod 3 mins 15 secs, Iron rod 4 mins 50 secs.

a) Which of these materials is the best conductor of heat?

b) Which of these materials is the worst conductor of heat?

c) What would Kiran and Mark need to keep the same in order to make it a FAIR TEST?

1. This simple circuit can be used to test whether an object is an electrical conductor. If it is, the bulb will light when the object is laid across the two bare wires.

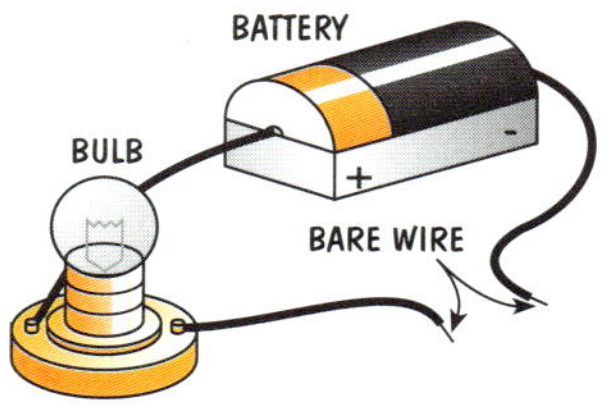

You have to decide whether the following objects are electrical conductors (will allow electricity through them) or electrical insulators (won't allow electricity through). Put a CIRCLE around the CONDUCTORS, and a CROSS through the INSULATORS.

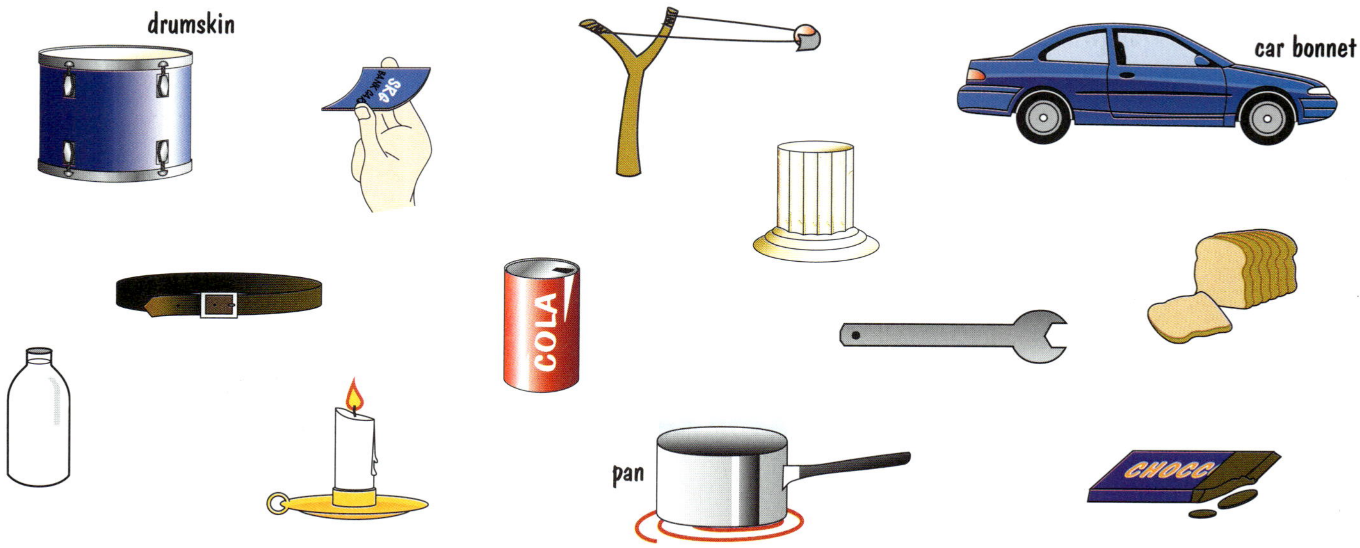

2. Label the diagram of the plug below showing those materials which are good CONDUCTORS in RED, and those which are good INSULATORS in BLUE.

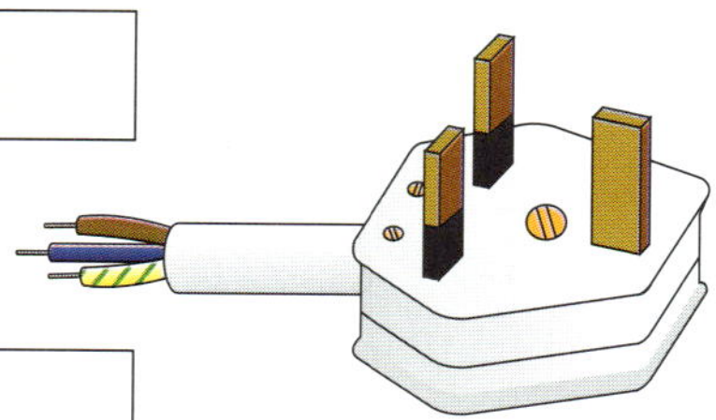

3. Name 5 household items in which a good electrical insulating material is important.

1. Complete the following crossword on "rocks".

CLUES DOWN

1. Hard rock made of crystals - not permeable.

3. Hard smooth rock made of crystals in layers. Not permeable and often used on a roof.

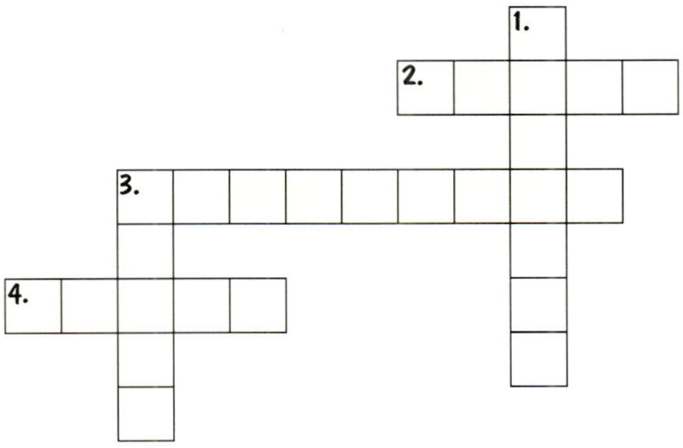

CLUES ACROSS

2. Hard smooth rock made of crystals in layers. Not permeable. Used for decoration when polished.

3. Crumbly permeable rock used sometimes for building.

4. Crumbly permeable rock often "seen with black boards".

2. If you look through your living room window you may not see any rocks at all. Try to explain why rocks aren't always visible.

3. Some pupils placed 3 different soil samples into fine mesh sieves as shown in the diagram.

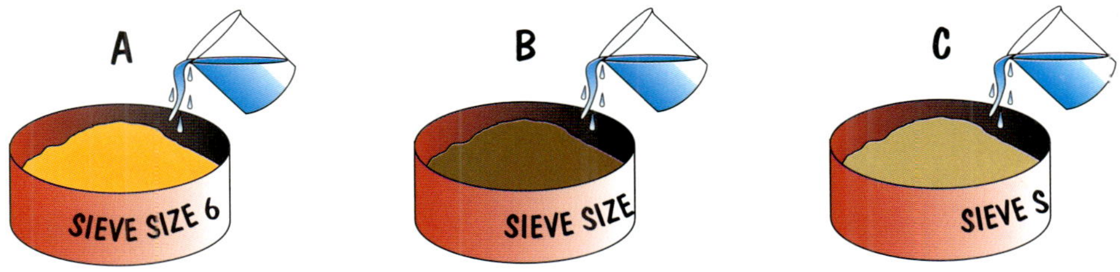

They weighed the sieves and soil, and poured water onto the soil and allowed it to run through into the sink. They weighed the sieves and soil again, and calculated the weight gained.
Here are their results: A gained 11 grams, B gained 16 grams, and C gained 13 grams.

a) In the space below, put these results into a suitable table and draw a bar chart of them on the squared paper.

b) Which of these soils is the most permeable?

c) What must be kept the same in this experiment in order to make it a FAIR TEST?

1. Say whether the following descriptions are describing SOLIDS, LIQUIDS or GASES.

a) Stay the same shape.

b) Keep the same volume and flow.

c) Take the shape of their whole container.

d) Don't flow.

e) Keep the same volume and take the shape of the bottom of their container.

f) Keep the same volume and the same shape.

g) Keep the same volume but don't keep the same shape.

h) Have no definite volume.

i) Keep the same volume and don't flow.

j) Flow and can have any volume.

2. Fill in the columns in the following table with everyday solids, liquids and gases.

SOLIDS	LIQUIDS	GASES

3. Explain why granulated sugar and flour 'flow' even though they are solids!

1. Fill in the gaps in the following passage ...

We use a ________ to measure temperature. Temperature is usually measured in ________ which is usually shown by the symbol ________ .

2. Estimate the temperature of the following things.

From the fridge

________ °C

Freshly made tea

________ °C

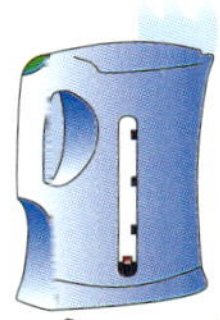

Steam from a kettle

________ °C

Surface of a small bulb

________ °C

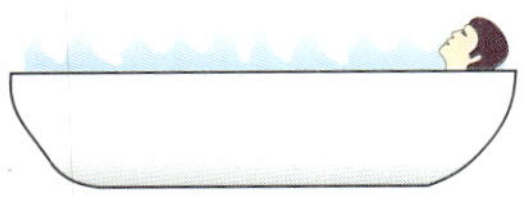

A bath of hot water

________ °C

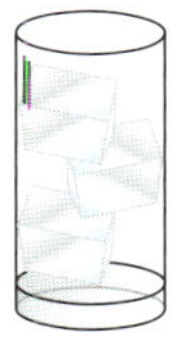

Ice just starting to melt

________ °C

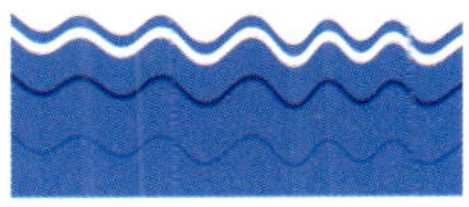

The sea around Britain in the summer

________ °C

Hot summer's day

________ °C

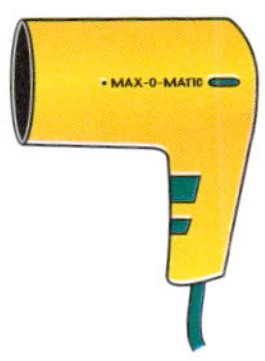

Hairdryer

________ °C

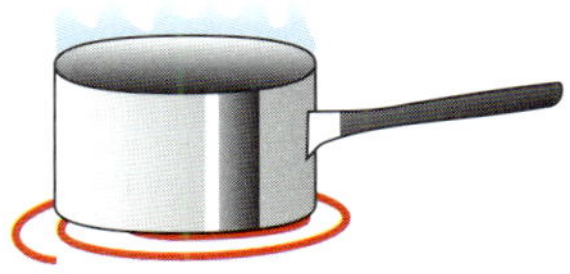

Pan of boiling water

________ °C

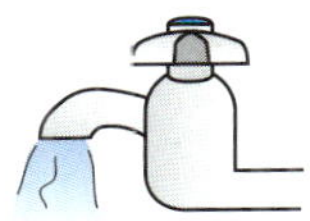

Cold water from the tap

________ °C

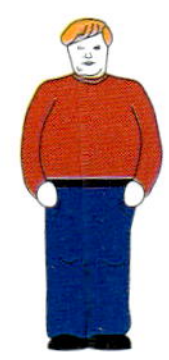

A human being

________ °C

3. Now put your estimates IN ORDER, STARTING WITH THE LOWEST in the form of a bar chart on the squared paper below.

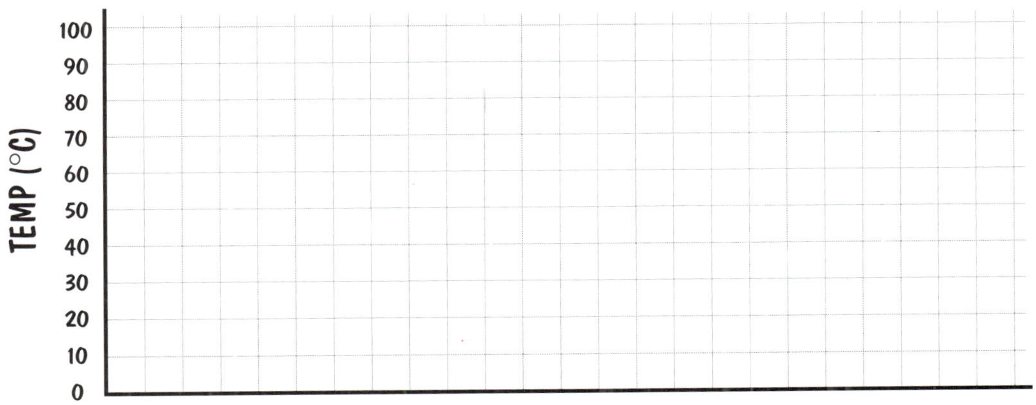

1. Look carefully at the following CHANGES and say whether they are REVERSIBLE or IRREVERSIBLE. Try to explain the reasons for your answer.

a) Adding water to sand and cement and leaving it for 12 hours.

This type of change is ______ because ______

______

b) Mending something with SUPERGLUE (ie. the change is in the glue!)

This type of change is ______ because ______

______

c) Pumping air into a balloon to make it bigger.

This type of change is ______ because ______

______

d) Heating wax and then pouring it into a mould to make a model.

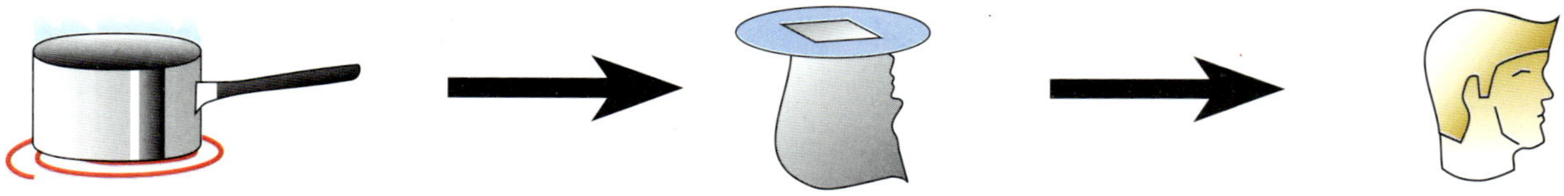

This type of change is ______ because ______

______

2. Write down in your own words what we mean by a REVERSIBLE CHANGE.

______

______

3. Give one example of a REVERSIBLE CHANGE.

______

1. Just like on the previous page, state whether the following changes are REVERSIBLE or IRREVERSIBLE. Try to explain the reasons for your answer.

a) Diluting concentrated orange squash.

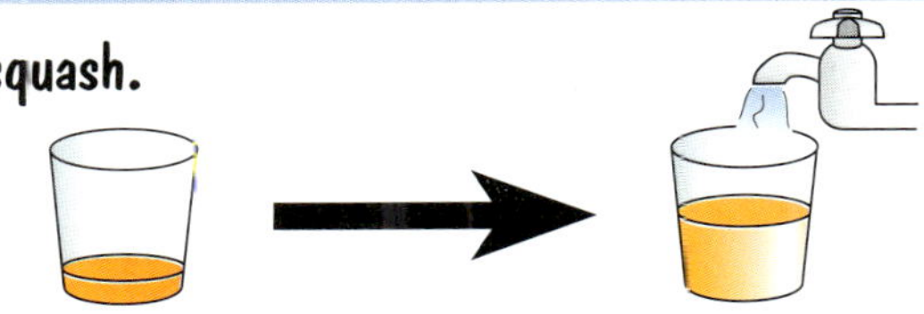

This type of change is ______ because ______

b) Burning a candle.

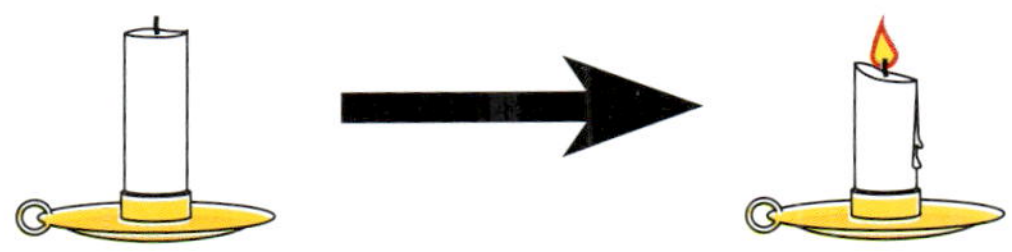

This type of change is ______ because ______

c) Heating a piece of steel until it glows.

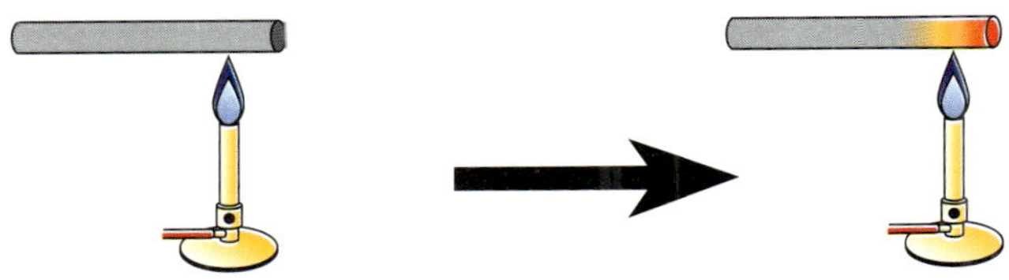

This type of change is ______ because ______

d) Setting off a firework.

This type of change is ______ because ______

2. Write down in your own words what we mean by an IRREVERSIBLE CHANGE.

3. Give one example of an IRREVERSIBLE CHANGE.

1. Write down the changes of state which are occurring for each of the letters A - D.

A	B	C	D

2. Steven and Nadia add several ice cubes to a beaker of water and take the temperature every 20 minutes. Their results are in the table below.

a) Plot these results accurately onto the squared paper in the form of a LINE GRAPH.

TIME (mins)	TEMP (°C)
0	15
20	5
40	5
60	10
80	14
100	18
120	19
140	19
160	19

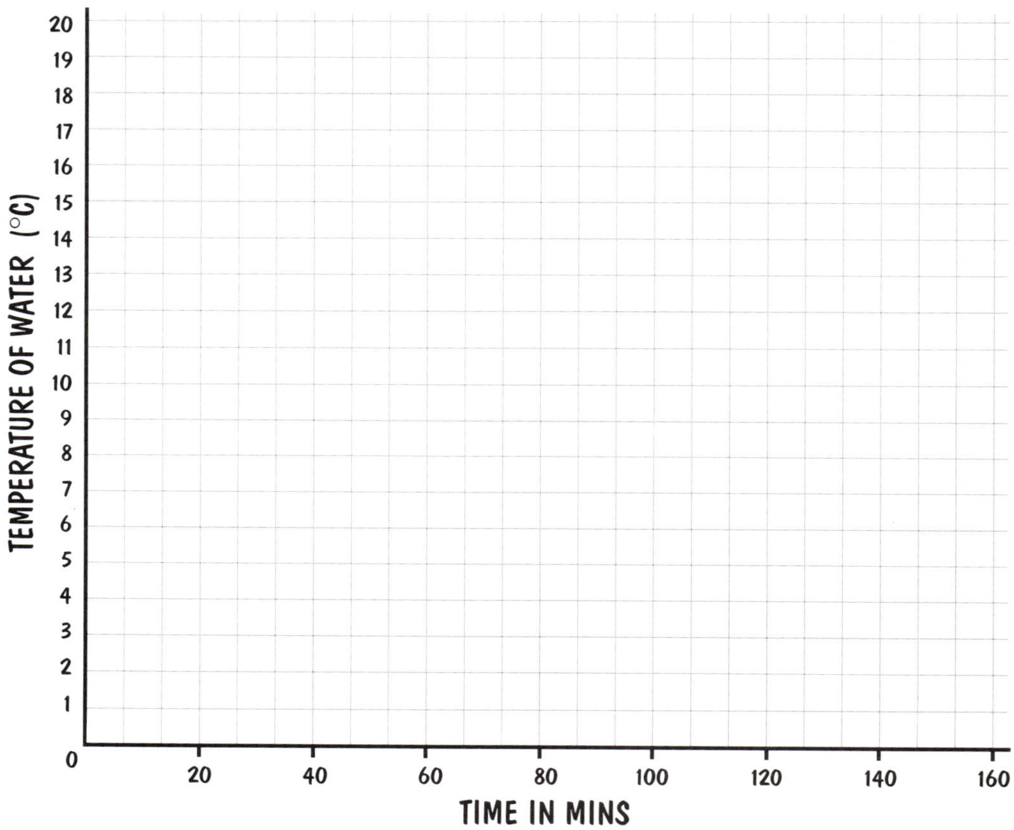

b) How many minutes passed before the ice melted?

c) How do you know this?

d) What was the temperature of the room in which they did this experiment?

1. Some pupils were investigating how the shape of the container could affect how quickly water evaporated from it. They placed 150cm³ of water into these three containers, and measured the volume of water in each of them after one week.

Here are the results they got.

a) In the spaces below the bar chart write in the letter of the container which that bar represents.

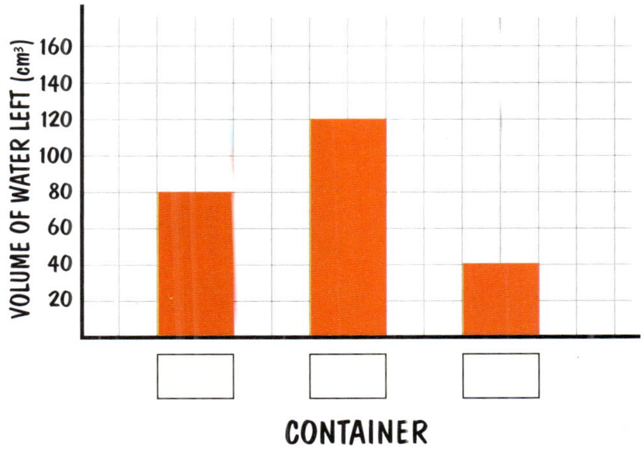

b) What do these results show?

c) What should the pupils have kept the same in order to make this a FAIR TEST?

2. The pupils now used three identical containers to investigate how temperature affects the speed of evaporation.

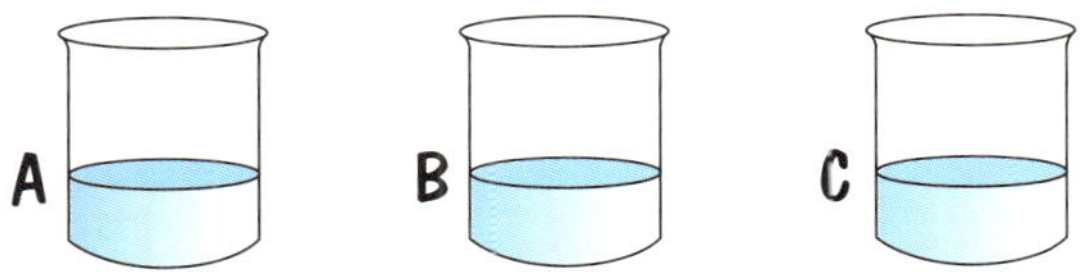

They placed 150cm³ into each beaker and placed each one in a different room at different temperatures. They measured the volume in each beaker after one week. Here are their results.

A = 100 cm³ B = 60 cm³ C = 80 cm³

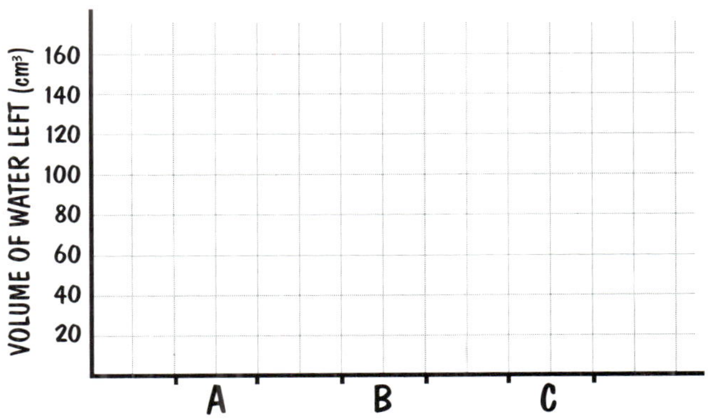

a) Plot these onto the squared paper in the form of a bar chart.

b) Which container had been in the hottest room?

c) Which container had been in the coldest room?

d) Explain your answers.

3. a) What is the name given to the process which is opposite to evaporation?

b) Give one example of this.

1. On the diagram of the water cycle below, write the following descriptions in the correct places.

CLOUDS BLOWN INLAND BY WIND	TRANSFER OF WATER BACK TO SEA	EVAPORATION (from seas, oceans, rivers, etc)	CONDENSATION OCCURS AND CLOUDS FORM	RAIN FALLS	SNOW FALLS

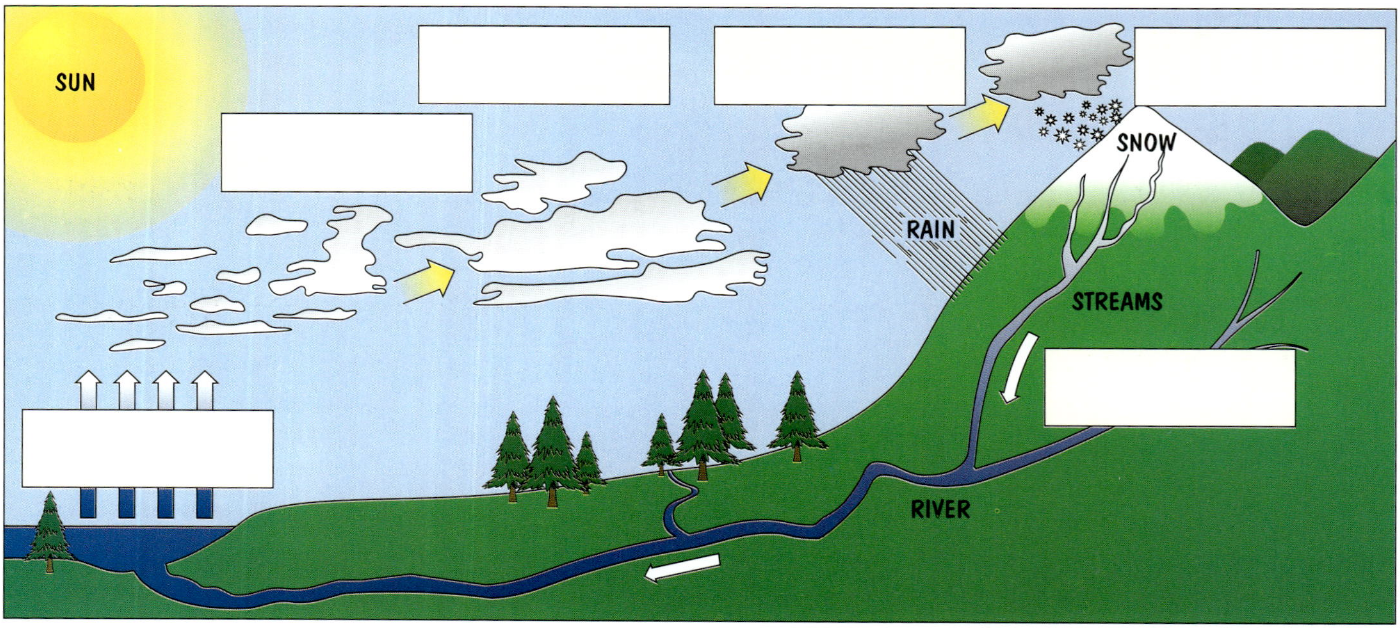

2. Try to write down three things which help evaporation to occur in this cycle.

a)

b)

c)

3. Try to write down one thing which helps condensation to occur in this cycle.

4. How can water be removed from the water cycle for long periods of time?

5. Why do you think the water cycle is so important to life on our planet?

1. Which of the following materials will dissolve in Water? Tick the ones that you think will, and cross the ones that you think won't.

☐	CLAY	☐	STONES	☐	SUGAR	☐	SALT
☐	CHALK	☐	BATH SALTS	☐	PEPPER	☐	SAND
☐	BAKING POWDER	☐	SHERBERT	☐	WAX	☐	POSTER PAINT

2. Harjinder was investigating how quickly sugar would dissolve in tea. He tried changing the temperature. These were his results.

TEMP (°C) of the tea	TIME (secs) taken to dissolve
10	40
20	36
30	27
40	19
50	15
60	12
70	8
80	7

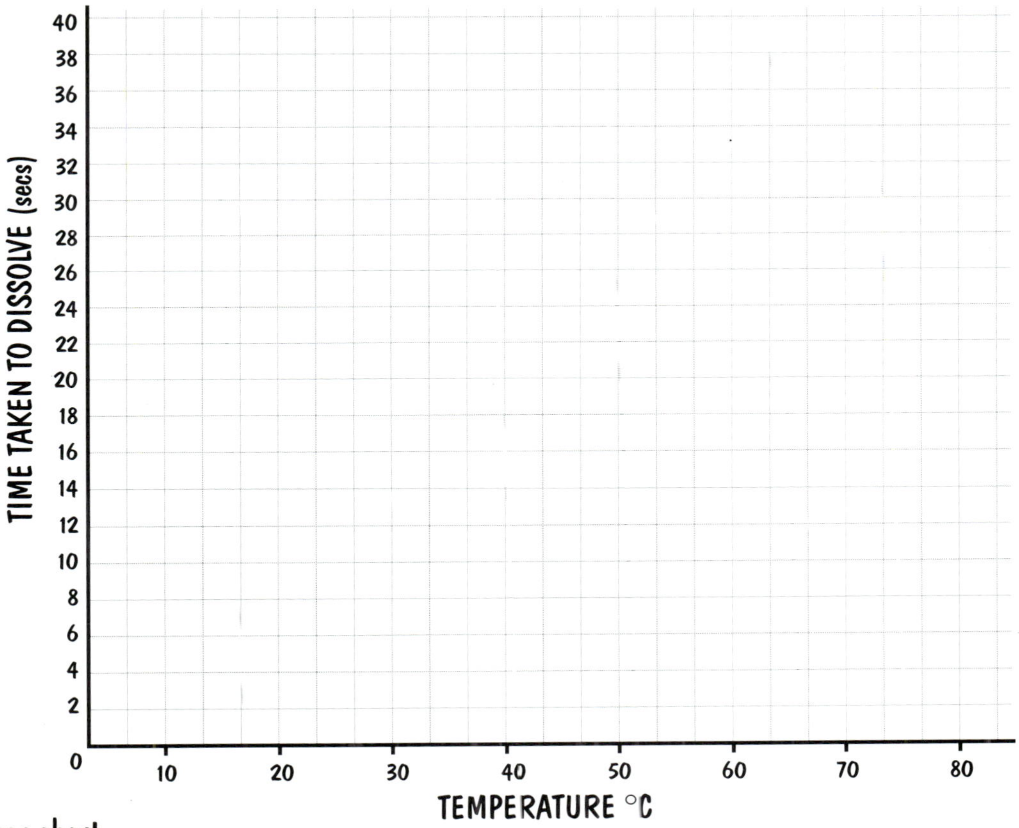

a) Plot these results as a bar chart.

b) Name 4 things which would have to be kept the same in order to make this a FAIR TEST.

1 ______

2 ______

3 ______

4 ______

1. Describe how you would separate the following ...

a) A pile containing 4 different sizes of dried bean.

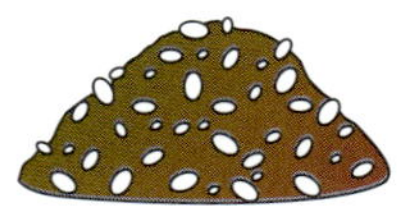

b) A beaker containing water and chalk powder.

c) A mixture of chalk and sugar.

d) Sugar dissolved in water.

e) A mixture of smarties and sand.

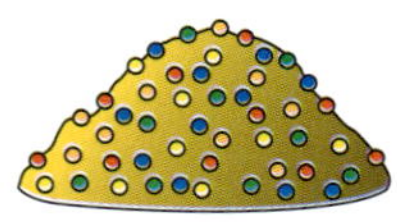

2. How would you find out how much solid was dissolved in pond water?

1. Below are a set of instructions you might follow if you wanted to separate a mixture of sand, gravel and salt. Unfortunately the instructions have been mixed up - you need to put them into the correct order in the spaces provided. (Use a pencil to begin with!)

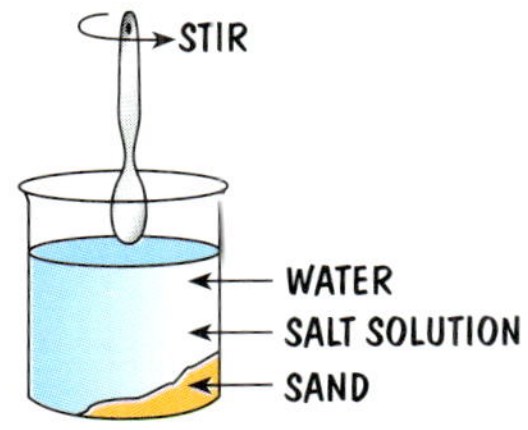

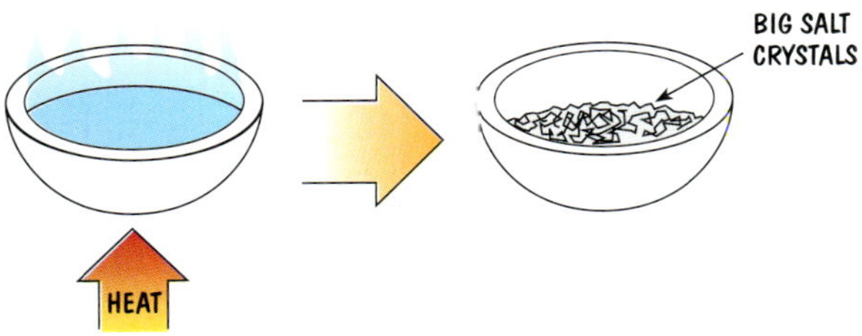

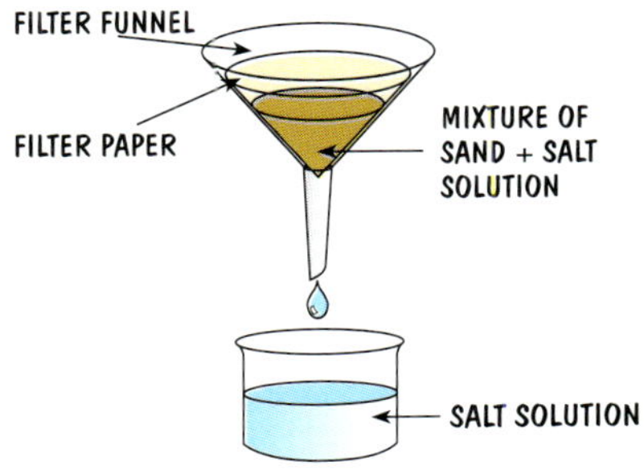

- Remove the gravel.
- Evaporate the solution that passes through the filter paper until it's completely dry.
- Sieve the mixture.
- When no more seems to be dissolving, filter the liquid through filter paper.
- Put the sand and salt into water and stir well.
- You will be left with salt.
- Remove the sand trapped by the filter paper.

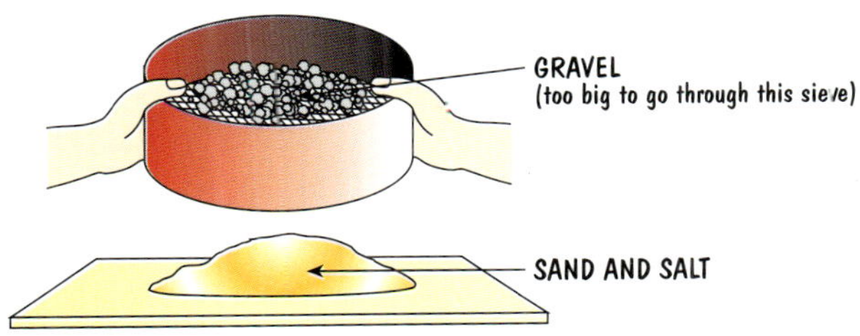

2. Why is it important to stir the sand and salt well?

1. Below are eight electrical appliances. Complete the sentences in the boxes.

a)

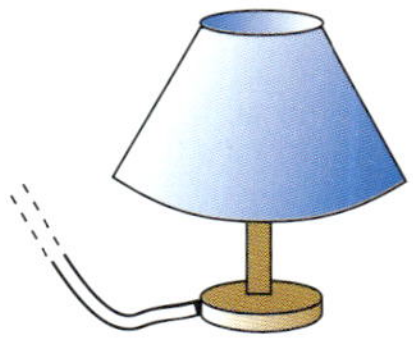

A table lamp needs electricity to produce

b)

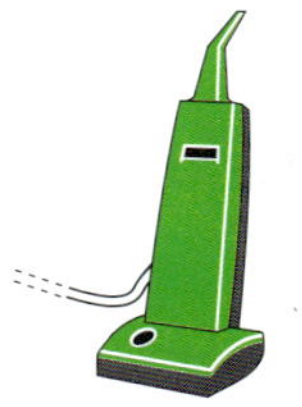

A vacuum cleaner needs electricity to produce

c)

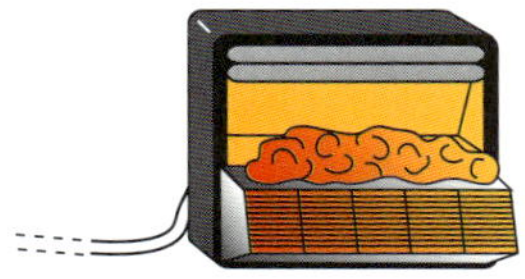

An electric fire needs electricity to produce

d)

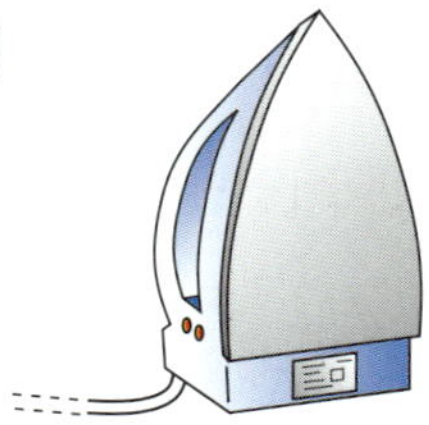

An iron needs electricity to produce

e)

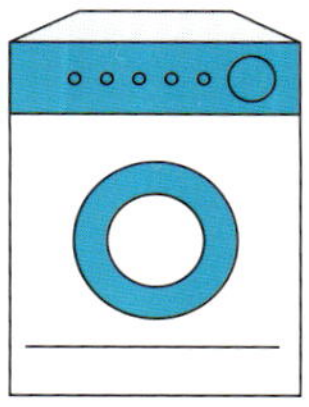

A tumble drier needs electricity to produce ______________

and ______________

f)

An alarm clock needs electricity to produce ______________

and ______________

g)

A television needs electricity to produce ______________

and ______________

h)

A cassette player needs electricity to produce ______________

and ______________

2. Complete the following boxes. The first one has been done for you.

		a)	b)	c)	d)	e)
WHAT IT LOOKS LIKE					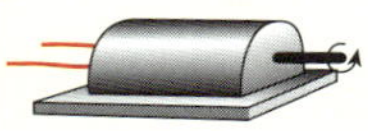	
WHAT IT IS	Bulb			Wires		Battery
WHAT IT DOES	Produces Light		Produces Sound			

3. Draw the symbol for:

a) Motor	b) Open switch	c) One battery	d) Wires
e) Buzzer	f) Closed switch	g) Bulb	h) Two batteries

1. Use the words in the boxes to fill in the gaps in the sentences below.

SWITCH	BREAK	ON	COMPLETE	ELECTRICITY	OFF	BREAK

A circuit which has a ____________ in it will not allow ____________ to flow through it. A device called a ____________ can be used to ____________ or ____________ a circuit so that other devices can be switched ____________ or ____________ .

2. The following circuits do not work. Explain why and what needs to be done to make them work.

a)

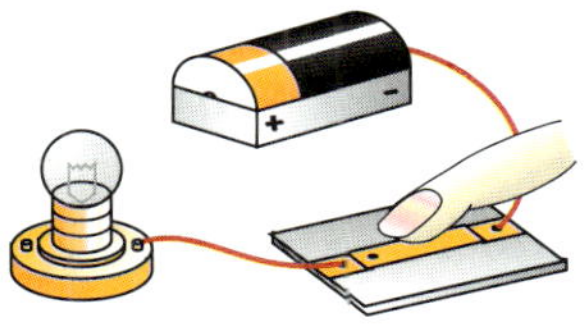

Why it doesn't work ____________

What needs to be done ____________

b)

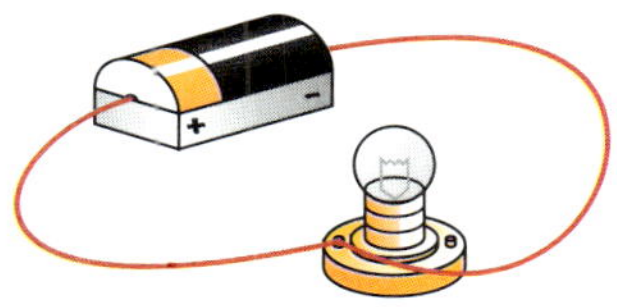

Why it doesn't work ____________

What needs to be done ____________

c)

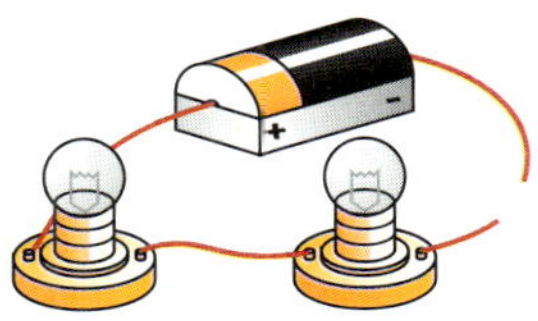

Why it doesn't work ____________

What needs to be done ____________

b)

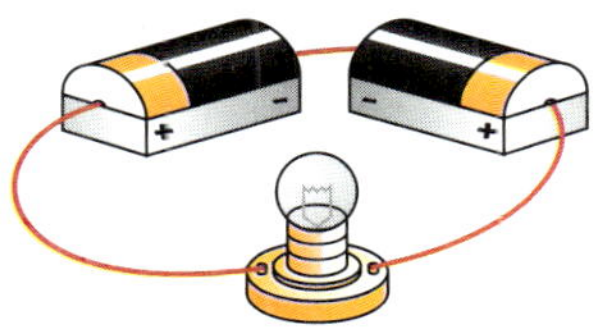

Why it doesn't work ____________

What needs to be done ____________

3. Make up and draw two other circuits that do not work. Explain why the circuit doesn't work and what needs to be done to make it work.

1. Draw the symbols for the following:

a) 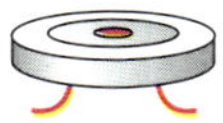

b) 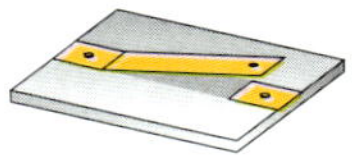

c) 

d) 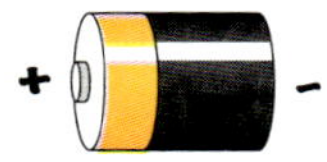

e) 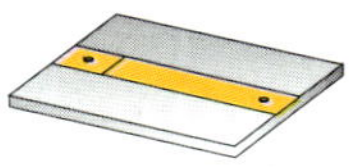

f) 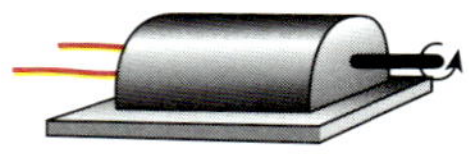

g) 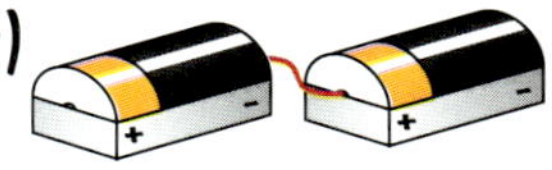

h) 

2. Draw a circuit diagram for each of the following circuits. Make sure you use a ruler.

a)

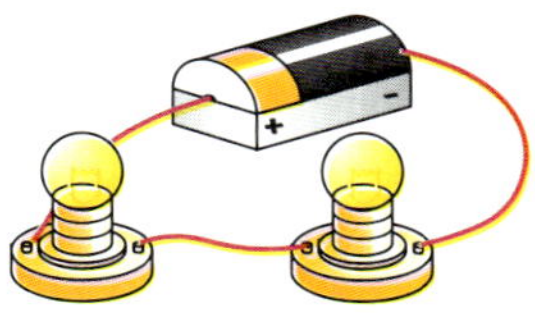

b)

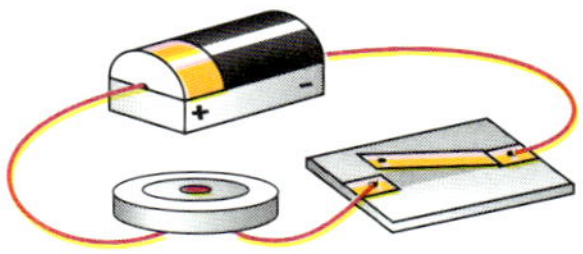

c)

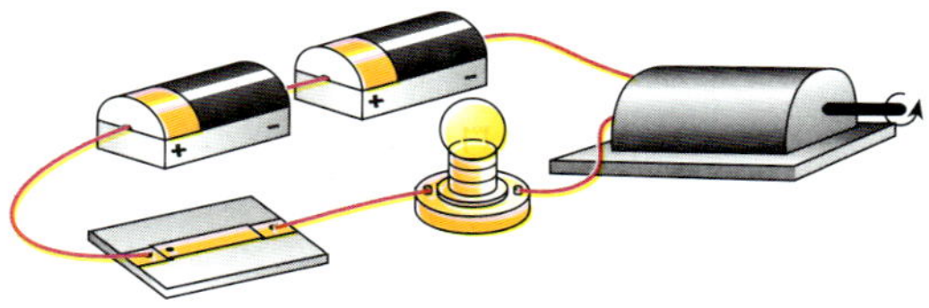

d)

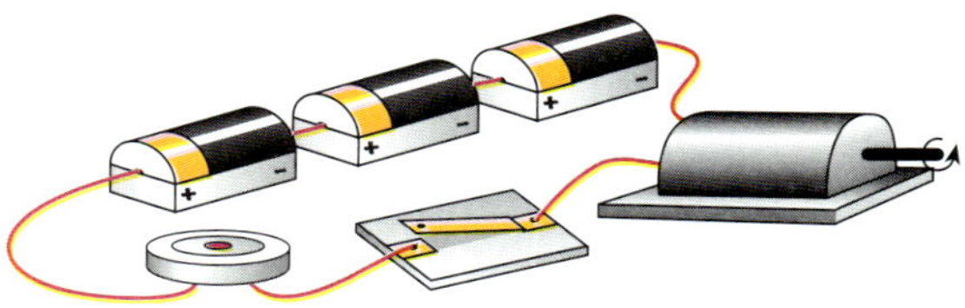

3. Below are two circuit diagrams. For each circuit diagram draw the circuit.

a)

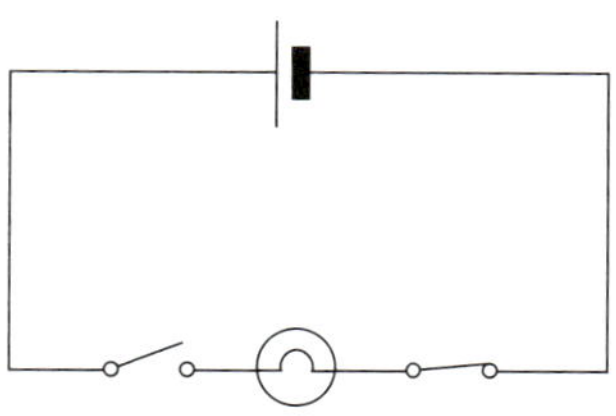

b)

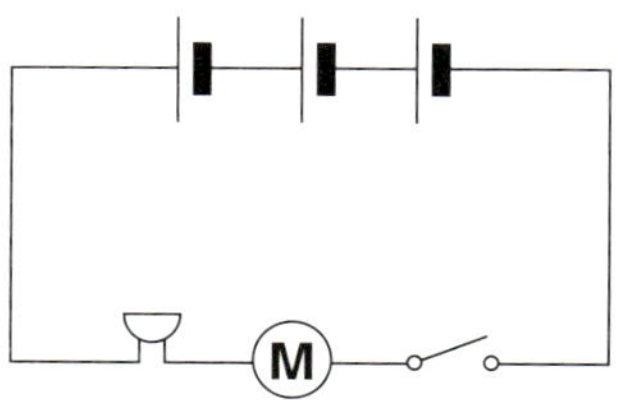

1. Fill in the gaps.

A flow of electricity in a circuit is called an _______________

Here is a simple circuit:

The brightness of the bulb depends on how much _______________ flows through the _______________. The greater the _______________, the _______________ the bulb.

2. Susan wants to investigate how changing the length of a certain wire in a circuit affects the brightness of a bulb. She sets up this simple circuit.

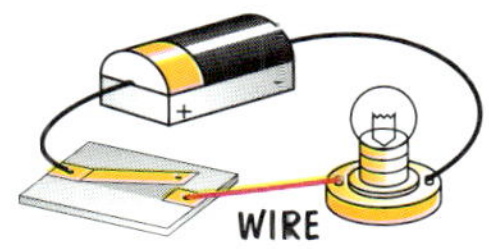

a) What must be kept the same if her investigation is to be a fair test?

____

b) She decides to double the length of wire. Explain why each of the following circuits is NOT a fair test for her investigation.

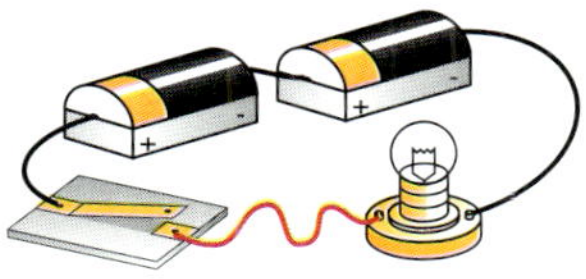

____

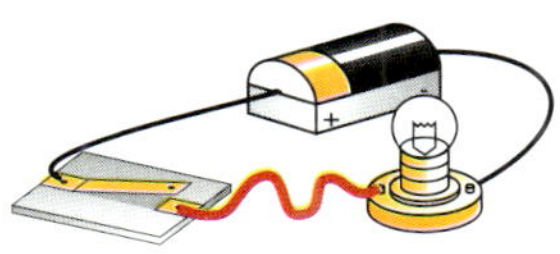

____

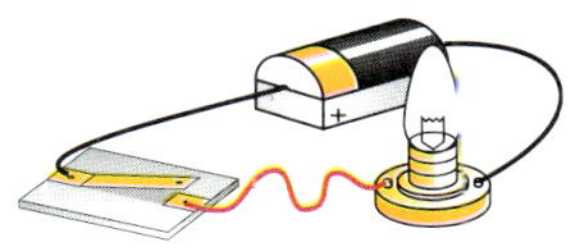

____

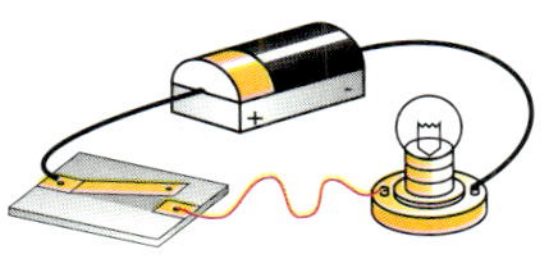

____

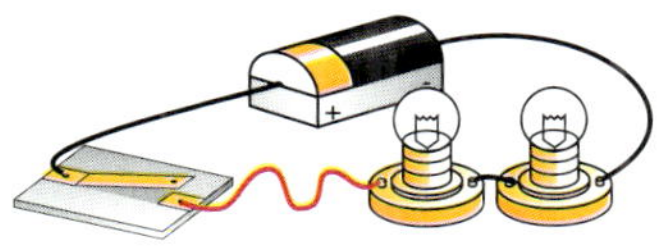

____

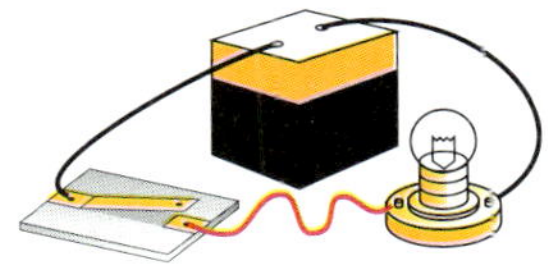

____

3. a) Susan carries out her investigation but unfortunately her results have become mixed up. Draw arrows to match up her results. One has been done for you.

Length of wire	60cm	100cm	40cm	120cm	20cm	80cm
Brightness of bulb	Bright	Very dim	Very, very bright	Very bright	Dim	Very, very dim

b) How does increasing the length of wire in her circuit affect the brightness of the bulb?

____

1. Use the words in the boxes to fill in the gaps in the sentences below.

STRAIGHT	NEWTONS	PUSH	ARROWHEAD	DIRECTION	END

A force is a ______ or a pull. A force is drawn as a ______ line with an ______ drawn at the ______ to show the ______ of the force. Forces are measured in ______ .

2. Fill in the following crossword with these words.

FORCE	NEWTONS	FRICTION	AIR RESISTANCE	WEIGHT	WATER RESISTANCE	UPTHRUST

When you have put the words in, write clues for each one in the spaces below.

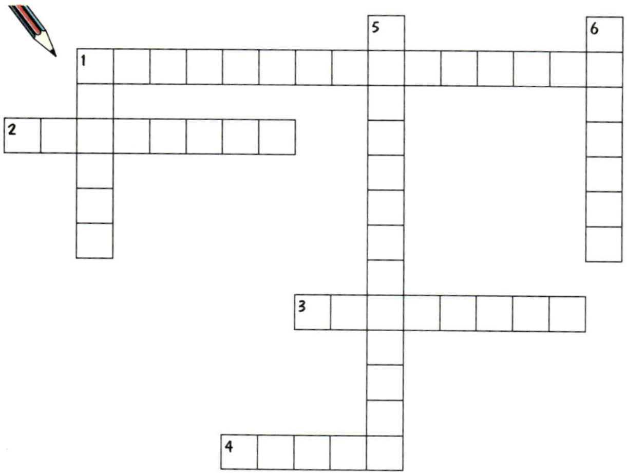

ACROSS:

1. ______
2. ______
3. ______
4. ______

DOWN

1. ______
5. ______
6. ______

3. Diagram a) shows a spring being stretched and diagram b) shows a spring being squeezed. On each diagram draw the forces which the spring produces on the hands.

a)

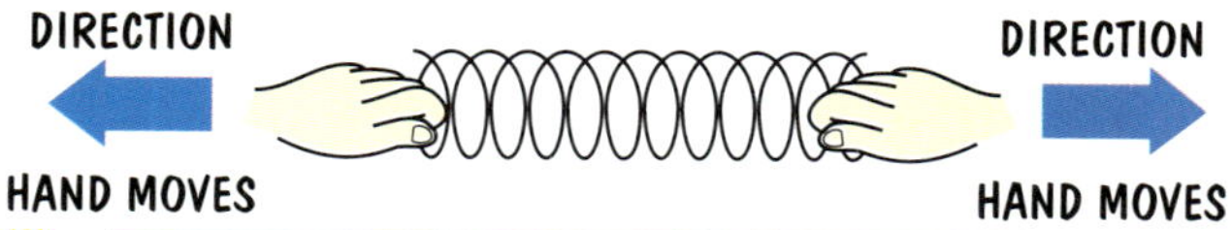

b)

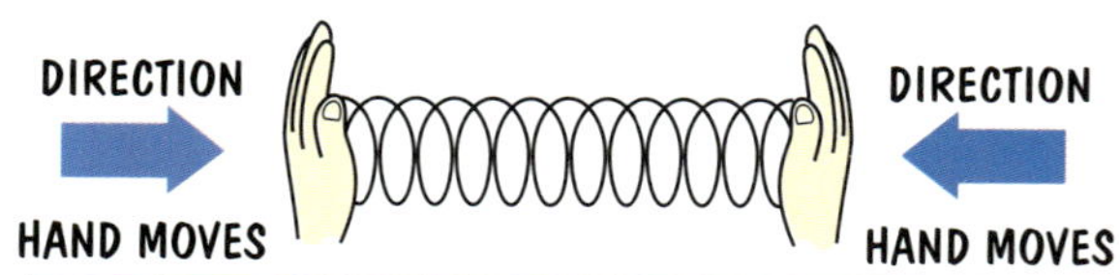

4. Which of the following diagrams shows the direction of the forces exerted on the hands by the elastic. Explain your answer.

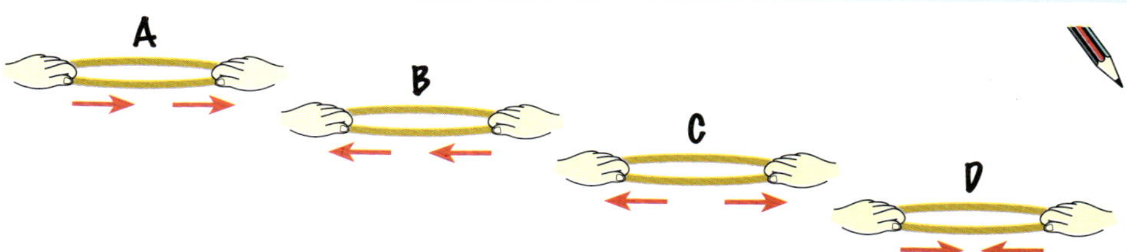

1. a) What is weight?

b) The weight of a girl in this country is 500N. What would happen to her weight if she goes to Australia? Explain your answer.

c) Weight is measured using a forcemeter. How does a forcemeter work?

d) What are the readings on the following forcemeters?

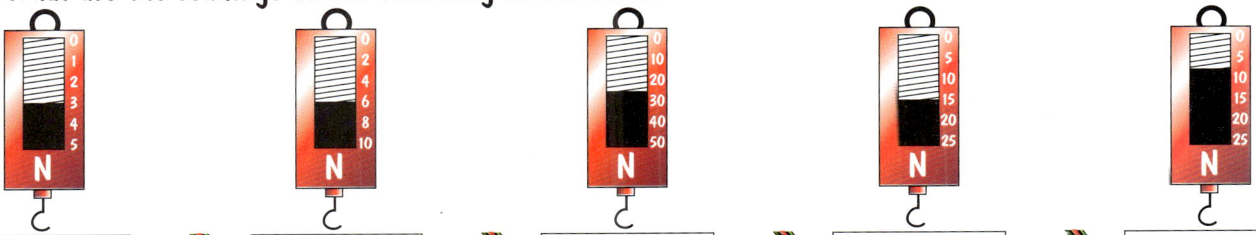

2. a) A simple forcemeter can be made using an elastic band. Four objects are hung from an elastic band as shown below.

Measure the length of each elastic band and then complete the bar graph below.

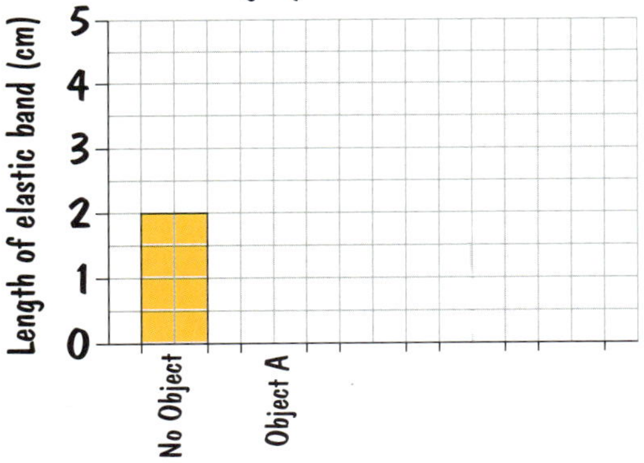

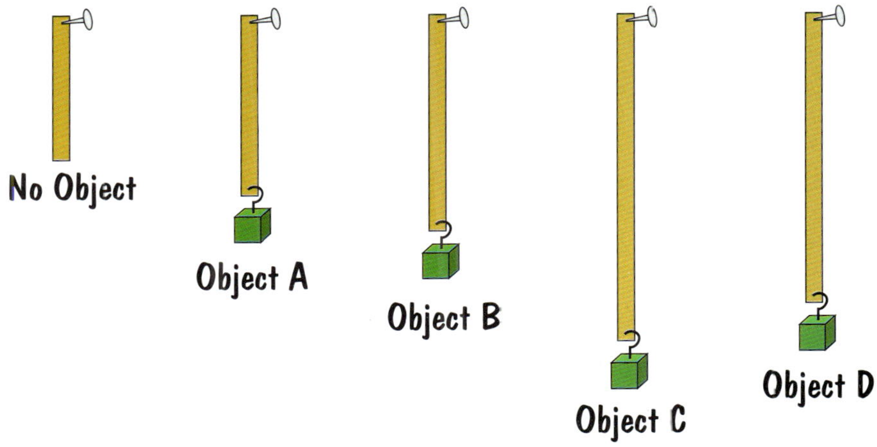

b) Which object is twice the weight of object B? Explain your answer.

c) Which object is five times the weight of object A? Explain your answer.

d) What would the length of the elastic band become if an object is hung from it that is twice the weight of object D?

1. On each of the following diagrams draw in the force of friction acting on each moving object. In the box beneath each diagram state whether the friction created is large or small.

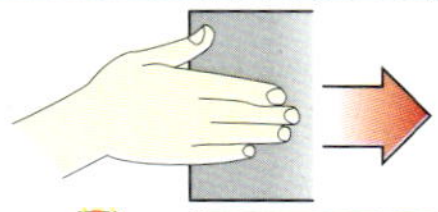

2. On each of the following diagrams draw in the force of air resistance acting on each moving object. In the box next to each diagram state whether the air resistance created is large or small.

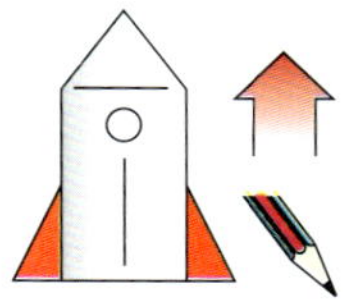

3. Jenny decided to investigate how different surfaces create different amounts of friction. A block of wood was pulled using a forcemeter as shown in the diagram. The reading on the forcemeter was taken just as the block started to move.

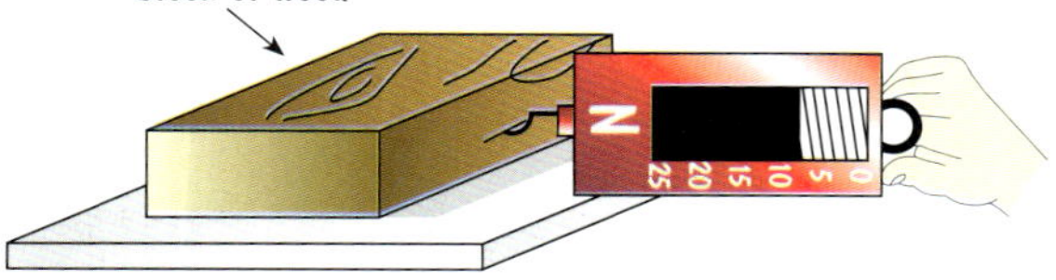

a) How will Jenny carry out a fair test?

b) Here are her results. Plot them as a bar graph.

Surface	Forcemeter reading
A	5N
B	3N
C	8N
D	1N
E	2N

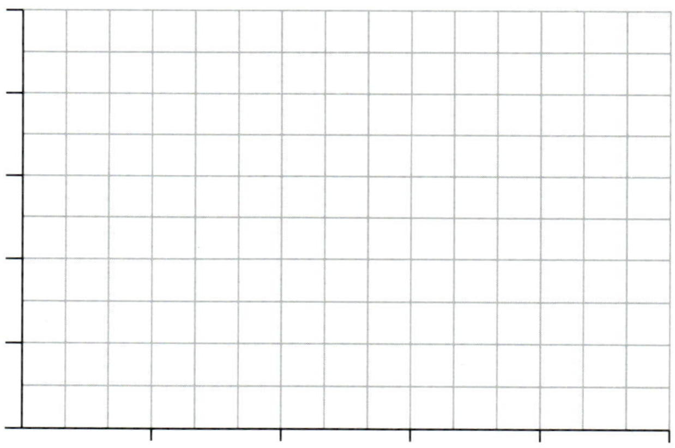

c) Which of these surfaces create:

i) The greatest friction

ii) The least friction

d) Oil is used to reduce friction between the moving parts of a car engine. Why does the oil reduce friction?

1. On each of the following diagrams draw in the force of water resistance on each moving object. In the box next to each diagram state whether the water resistance created is large or small.

Dolphin is moving in this direction

Submarine is moving in this direction

Diver is moving in this direction

2. Freya wants to investigate how the shape of a piece of plasticine affects how fast it falls through wallpaper paste.

a) What else does Freya need for her investigation?

b) What is Freya going to measure during her investgation?

c) How will Freya make sure that she carries out a fair test?

d) In the space opposite draw four possible plasticine shapes which Freya may use. Label them 1, 2, 3 and 4.

e) Which of the above shapes do you think will fall the fastest? Explain your answer.

f) Which of the above shapes do you think will fall the slowest? Explain your answer.

3. A forcemeter is used to weigh a ball in air. The reading on the forcemeter is 6N. The ball is now put into water.

a) Which of the following forcemeter readings is now correct. Tick a box.

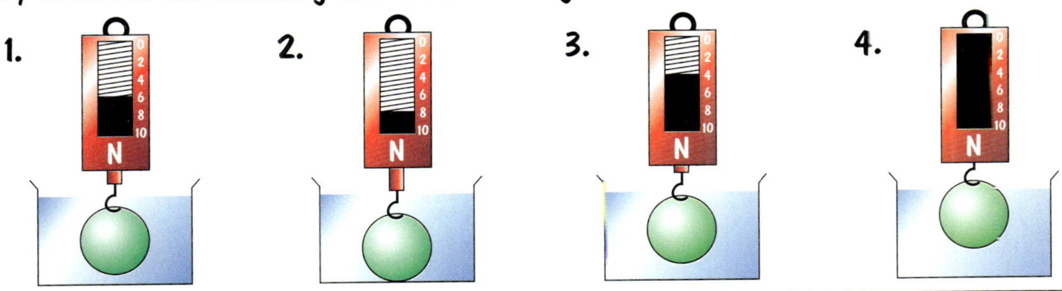

Forcemeter 1	
Forcemeter 2	
Forcemeter 3	
Forcemeter 4	

b) Explain your answer.

c) If the ball above had floated when put into the water, which of the above forcemeter readings would now be correct.

d) Explain your answer.

1. Which of the following materials are attracted to a magnet? If they are attracted put a ✓ in the box, if they are not attracted put a ✗. The first one has been done for you.

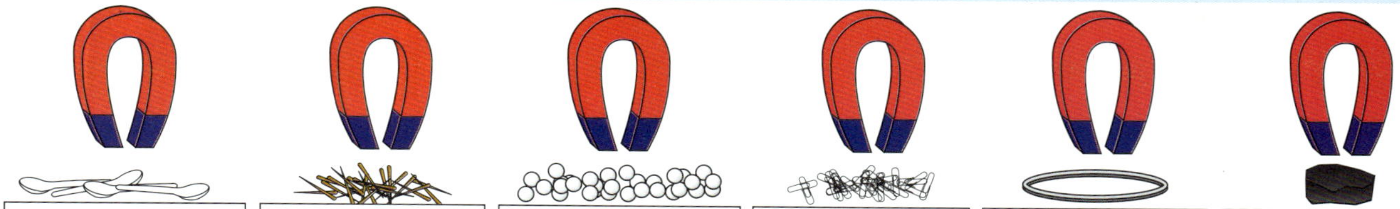

Plastic Spoons	Wooden Toothpicks	Polystyrene Balls	Steel Paper Clips	Iron Ring	Piece of Coal
✗					

2. Jimmy wants to investigate the strength of four magnets by finding out how many steel pins each magnet can pick up.

a) How would Jimmy make sure that he carries out a fair test?

b) Jimmy gets the following results:

Magnet	Number of steel pins picked up
A	2
B	3
C	5
D	1

Draw a bar graph to show the results.

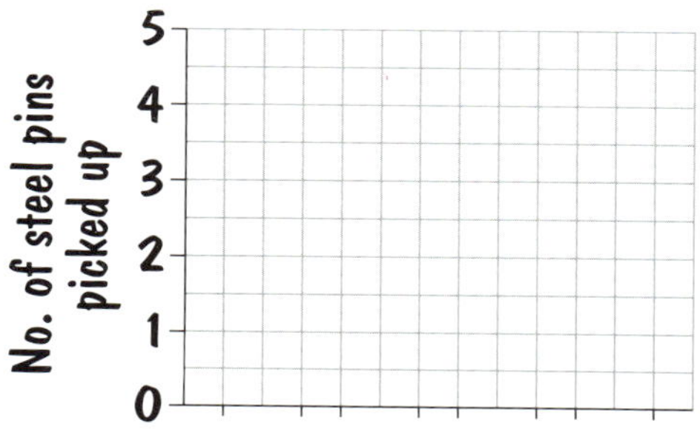

c) Which is the strongest magnet?

d) Explain your answer.

3. Fill in the following crossword with these words.

NORTH	POLES	MAGNETS	NICKEL	STEEL	MAGNETISM	COBALT	SOUTH	IRON

When you have put the words in, write clues for each one in the spaces below.

ACROSS

1.

2.

3.

4.

5.

DOWN

1.

6.

7.

8.

1. Which of the following are sources of light? Tick those that are.

MIRROR	STAR	MOON	EYES	TORCH	ICE	GLASS	SUN

2. a) What is a shadow?

b) Complete the following diagrams to show the shadow formed on the screen.

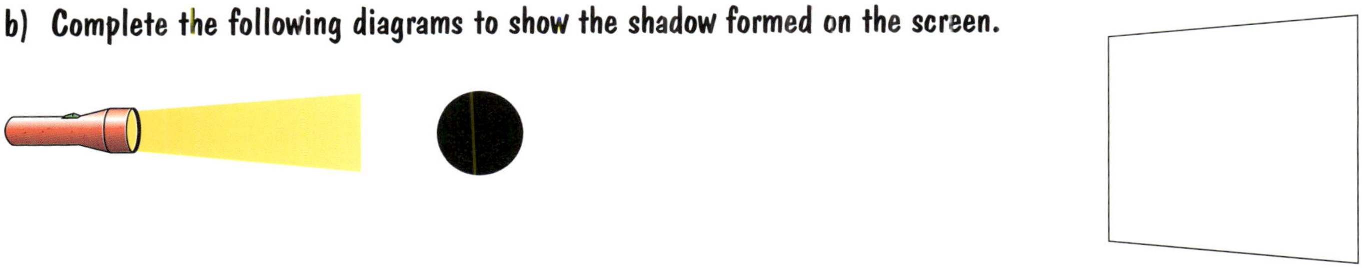

3. Wayne carried out an investigation to find out how the distance from the object to the screen affected the height of the shadow formed.

a) What must be kept the same if he is carrying out a fair test?

b) Here are his results.

Distance from object to screen	Height of Shadow
20cm	4cm
40cm	8cm
50cm	10cm
80cm	16cm

Plot the points on the graph opposite. The first point has been done for you.
Draw a straight line passing through all the points.

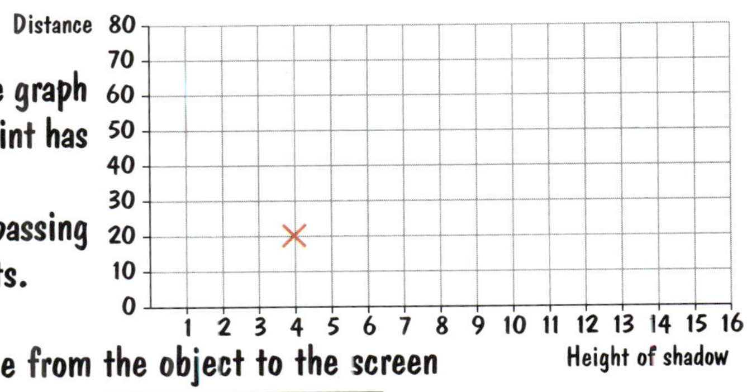

c) What is the height of the shadow when the distance from the object to the screen is 60cm? and then 75cm?

d) How does the distance from the object to the screen affect the height of the shadow formed?

1. A beam of light is shone on to a mirror. Put a tick next to the reflected beam which is correct. Below each diagram complete the simple diagram of the reflection. Make sure you use a protractor.

a)

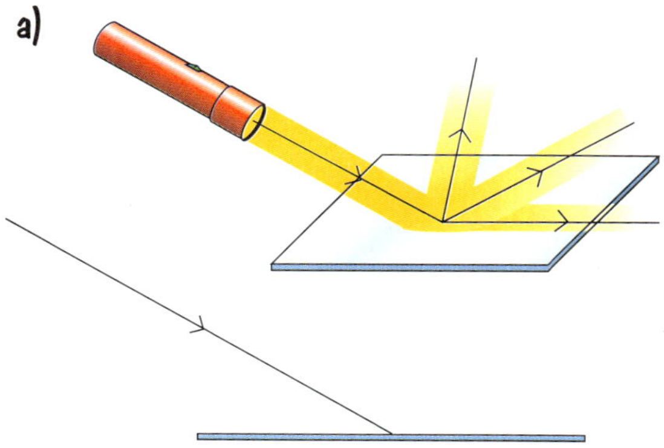

b)

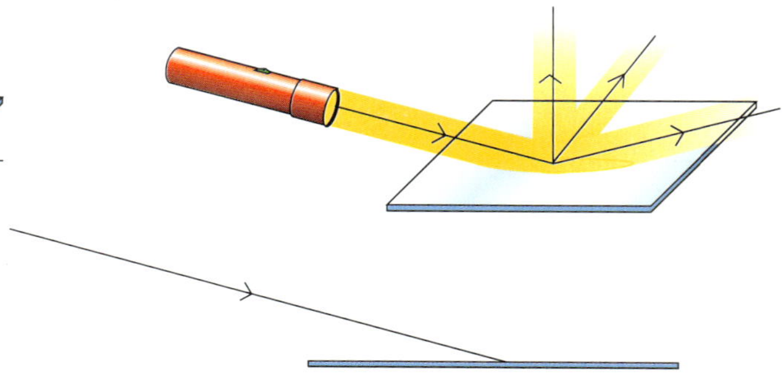

2. a) What is a periscope?

b) Below are four diagrams of a periscope in use. One of the diagrams is correct. Put a tick in the box underneath the diagram. The other diagrams are incorrect. In the box underneath each diagram explain why.

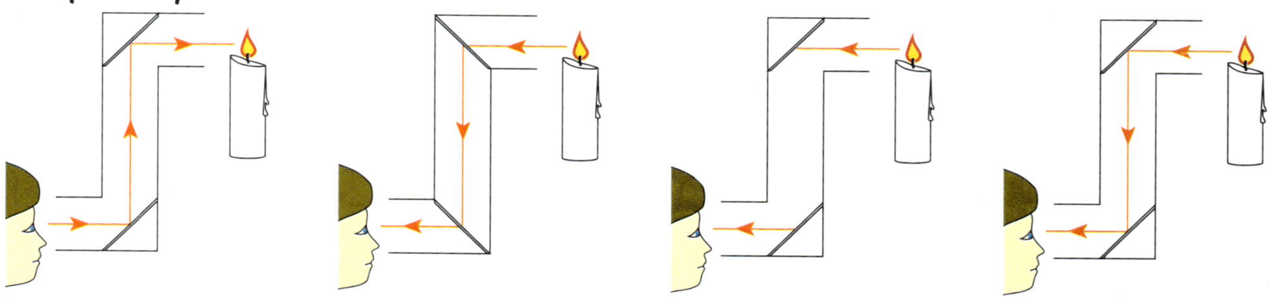

3. Explain why ...

a) You can see the Sun.

b) You can see the Moon.

c) You can see objects in a mirror.

1. Sound is produced when an object or material is made to vibrate. Which part of the following "objects" are vibrating to produce sound?

a) A bee buzzing.

b) A boy talking.

c) A girl blowing a 'raspberry.'

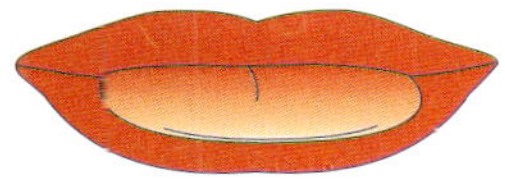

d) A radio.

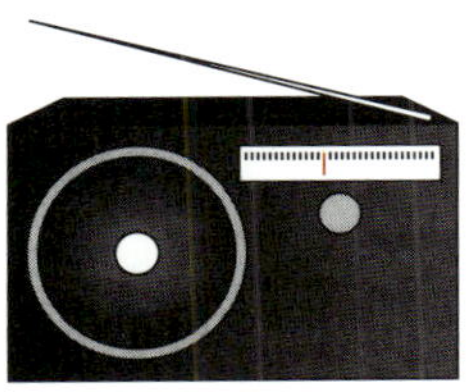

e) A boy walking on a wooden floor.

f) A girl tapping a window.

2. Hard and soft materials have different effects on sound.

a) Materials that are not very good at muffling sound are usually ______ materials.

b) Why is it important that we prevent too much sound reaching our ears?

c) Name 5 objects or materials in your bedroom at home that are very good at muffling sound and 5 objects which are not good at muffling sound.

VERY GOOD AT MUFFLING SOUND	NOT VERY GOOD AT MUFFLING SOUND
1.	1.
2.	2.
3.	3.
4.	4.
5.	5.

3. Complete the crossword.

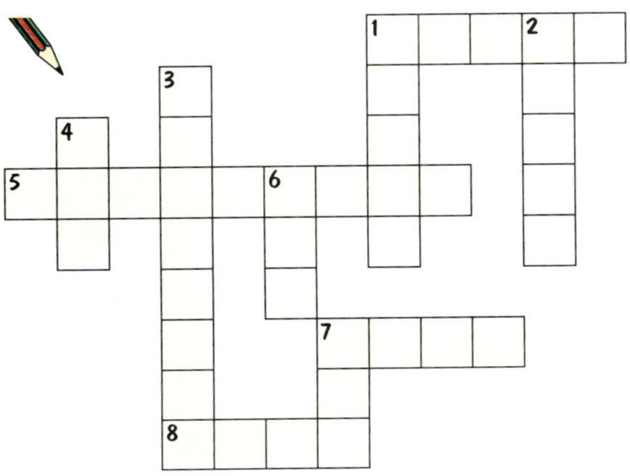

CLUES ACROSS

1. This is produced when an object vibrates.
5. Moving forwards and backwards quickly.
7. A material that is not very good at muffling sound.
8. A material that is very good at muffling sound.

CLUES DOWN

1. A hard material.
2. People who work in ______ places wear ear protection.
3. People wear these to stop sound reaching their ears.
4. Sounds pass through this for us to hear them.
6. You need to do this to a tuning fork to make it vibrate.
7. You need to do this to a drumskin to make it vibrate.

1. Simon investigated pitch by doing this simple experiment. A ruler was clamped to the end of a table.

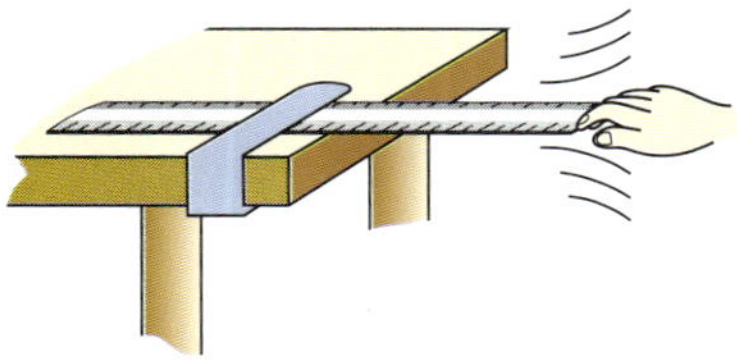

If you PLUCK the ruler you will hear a sound of a 'CERTAIN PITCH".

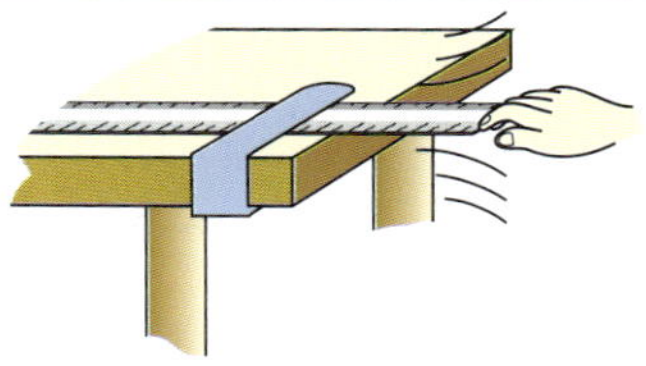

A SHORTER LENGTH and you will hear a sound of a 'HIGHER PITCH'.

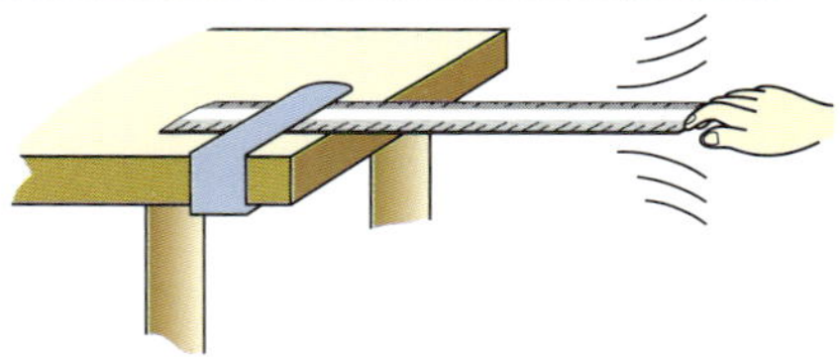

A LONGER LENGTH and you will hear a sound of a 'LOWER PITCH'.

Simon was now given five different tuning forks as shown below. Tuning forks make a sound when the two arms are tapped causing them to vibrate.

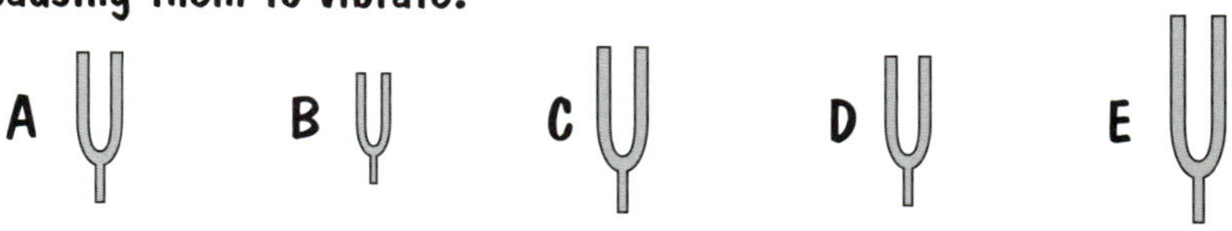

If you use the same idea as the vibrating ruler:

a) Which tuning fork would produce sound with the highest pitch. Explain your answer.

b) Which tuning fork would produce sound with the lowest pitch. Explain your answer.

2. a) What is loudness?

b) How would you increase the loudness of the sound produced by a tuning fork?

3. Amy sets up the following experiment where a ruler is clamped to a table and each time the length of the ruler is different. Amy then plucks each ruler to produce a sound.

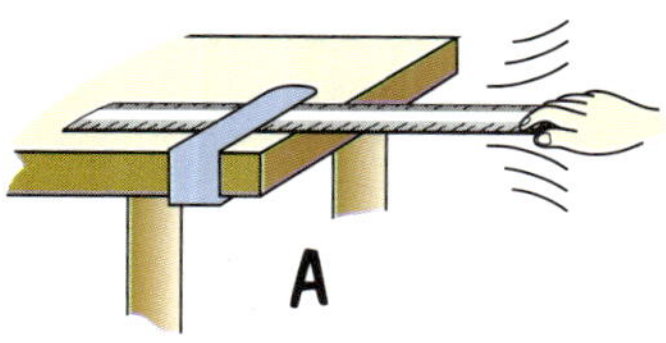

A

Amy plucks the ruler.

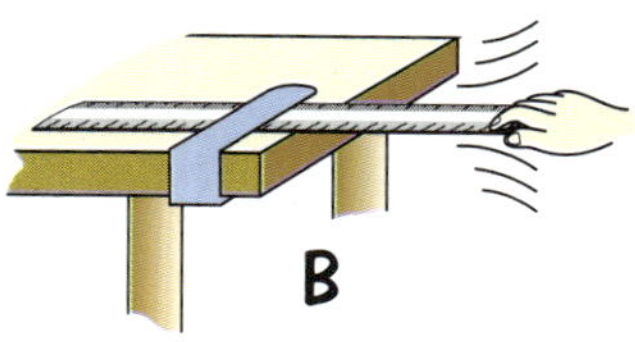

B

Amy plucks the ruler harder.

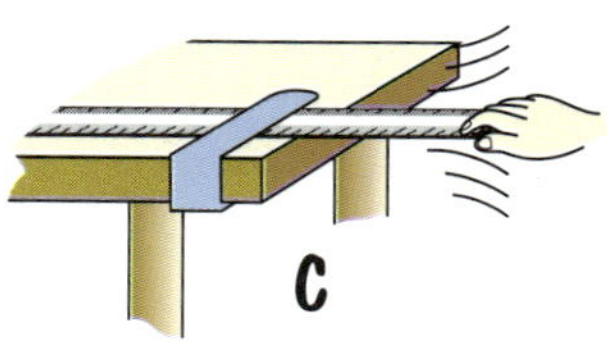

C

Amy plucks the ruler more gently.

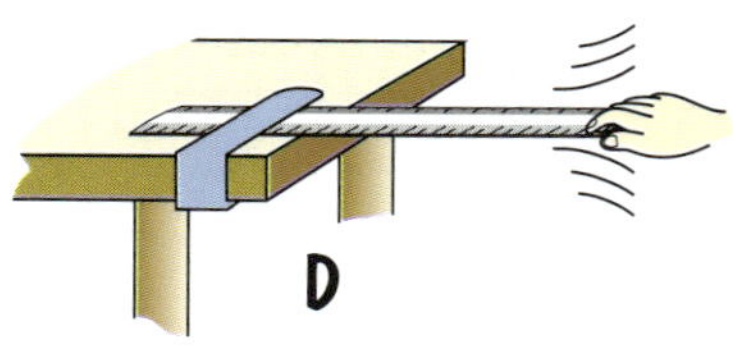

D

Amy plucks the ruler much harder.

a) What affect does plucking the ruler harder and more gently have on the sound produced? Explain your answer.

b) Which ruler would produce the highest pitch and the quietest sound? Explain your answer.

c) Which ruler would produce the lowest pitch and the loudest sound? Explain your answer.

1. Sabrina wants to investigate how the length of a guitar string affects the pitch of the sound it produces when it is plucked. She sets up the following experiment.

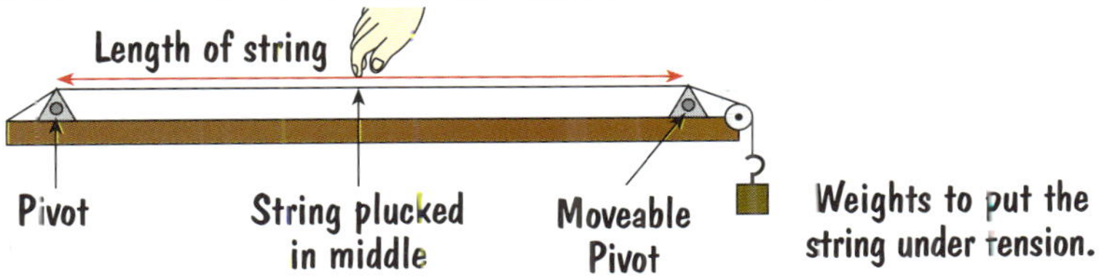

a) How would Sabrina make sure that she carries out a fair test?

b) Sabrina gets the following results but unfortunately her results have become mixed up. Draw arrows to match up her results. One has been done for you.

LENGTH OF WIRE	10cm	70cm	50cm	90cm	30cm
PITCH OF SOUND	MEDIUM	HIGH	VERY LOW	VERY HIGH	LOW

c) How could Sabrina increase the pitch of the sound without altering the length of the string?

d) How could Sabrina increase the loudness of the sound produced by the string?

2. David decides to make his own wind instrument by putting water into six bottles as shown below. Sound is produced if you blow across the top of the bottle.

a) Which bottle would produce sound with the lowest pitch?

b) Which bottle would produce sound with the highest pitch?

c) Which two bottles would produce sound with the same pitch? Explain your answer.

3. Opposite are five drums.

a) Which drum would produce sound with the lowest pitch? Explain your answer.

b) How is it possible for drum A and drum E to produce sound of the same pitch

1. In the space below draw a fully labelled diagram of the Sun, Earth and Moon including their orbits.

2. a) How long does it take the Earth to orbit the Sun?

   b) How long does it take the Moon to orbit the Earth?

   c) In the time it takes the Earth to orbit the Sun once, how many orbits (to the nearest whole number) will the Moon have made of the Earth?

3. a) Below are the four faces we see of the Moon as it orbits the Earth. They are all mixed up.

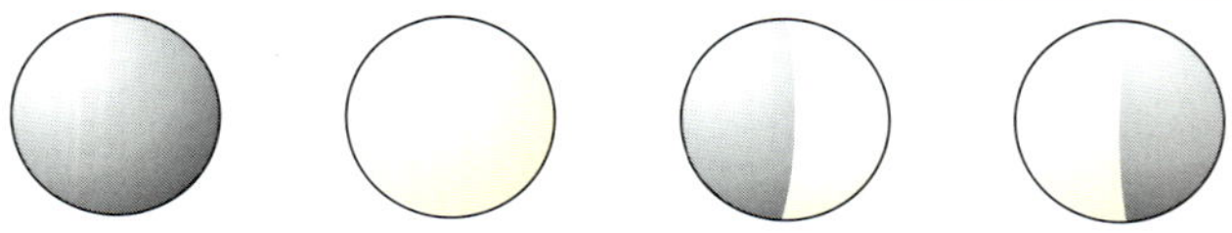

Complete the following diagram by drawing in each circle the face shown by the Moon. One is done for you.

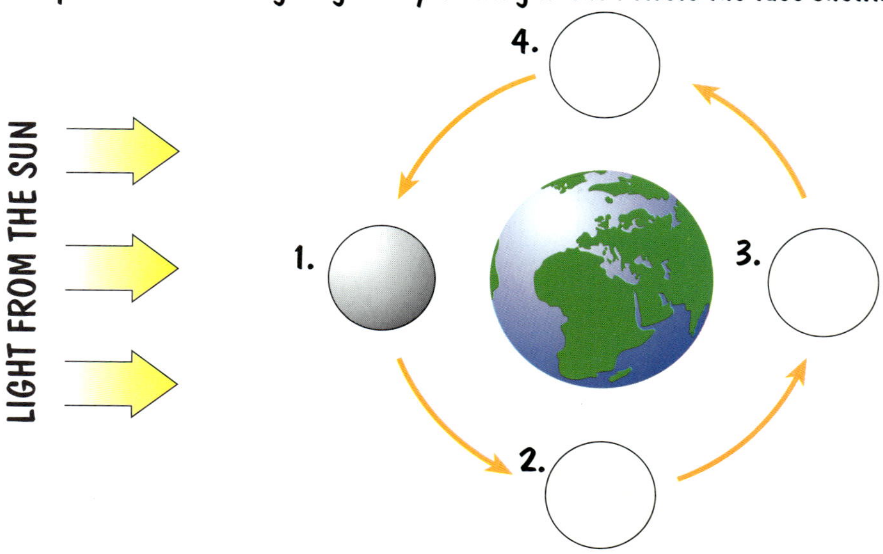

   b) How long does it take the Moon to orbit the Earth from position 1 to position 3?

   c) How long does it take the Moon to orbit the Earth from position 1 to position 4?

1. Jack and Tony are having an argument about the shape of the Earth.

Who do you think is correct? Explain your answer.

2. The Earth is roughly 4 times wider than the Moon and the Sun is roughly 100 times wider than the Earth.

a) If the width of the Moon is 1m, what is the width of i) the Earth?

ii) the Sun?

b) If the width of the Earth is <u>your height</u>, what is the width of i) the Sun?

ii) the Moon?

3. Here are the names of 6 famous astronomers and scientists who have had ideas about the shape and position of the Earth.

PYTHAGORAS	COPERNICUS	NEWTON
ARISTARCHUS	GALILEO	PTOLEMY

Use these names to make up your own wordsearch in the grid opposite and give it to your best friend to do.

1. Complete the following sentences using the following:

AXIS	DAYTIME	24 HOURS	ROTATION	NIGHT-TIME	SPINNING

As the Earth moves around the Sun it is also ________ around on its ________ . The Earth completes one ________ every ________ . The part of the Earth which is facing towards the Sun is in ________ and the part of the Earth facing away from the Sun is in ________ .

2. a) The table below gives the number of daily hours of daytime this country has over a period of twelve months.

MONTH	January	February	March	April	May	June
NUMBER OF HOURS OF DAYTIME	8.5	10	12	14	15.5	16.5

MONTH	July	August	September	October	November	December
NUMBER OF HOURS OF DAYTIME	16	14.5	13	10.5	9	8

Draw a bar graph to show the table. The first one has been done for you.

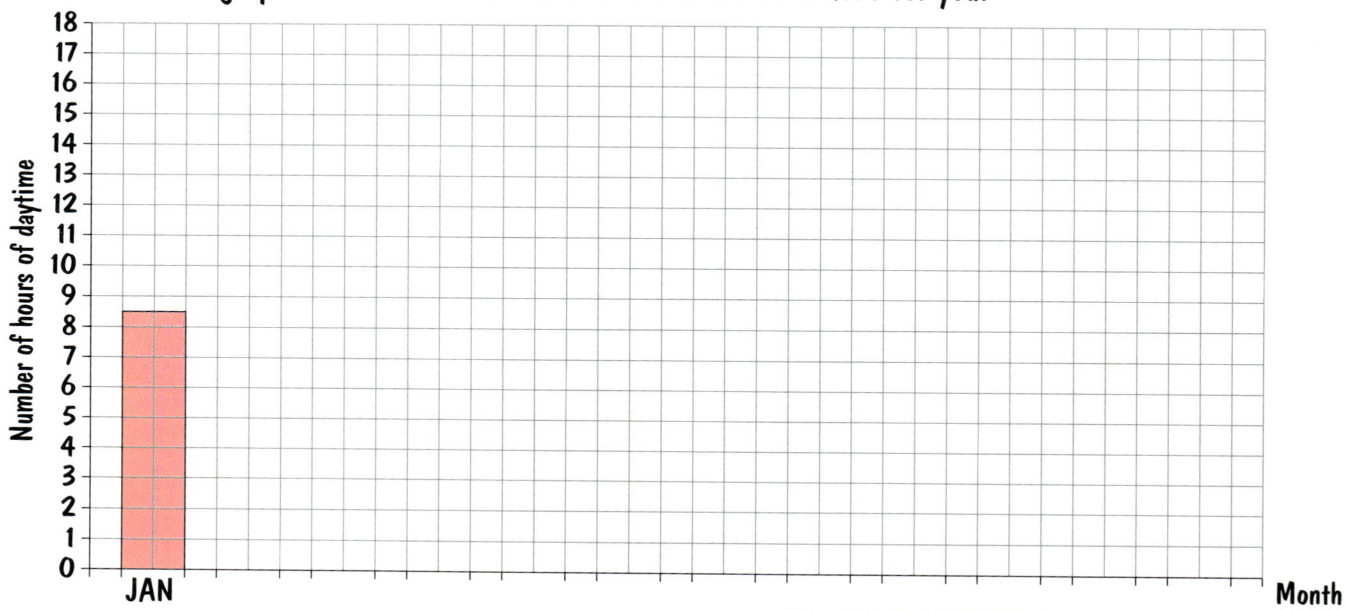

b) Which month has the most number of hours of daytime? ________

c) Which month has the least number of hours of daytime? ________

d) Which month has the same number of hours of daytime as night-time? ________

e) Which month has 15 hours of night- time? ________

3. The longest day of the year i.e. the day which has the greatest number of hours of daytime is June 21st. Which is the shortest day i.e. the day that has the least number of hours of daytime (think about it).

____

1. The line graph below shows the sunrise times for the first day of every month over a period of 12 months.

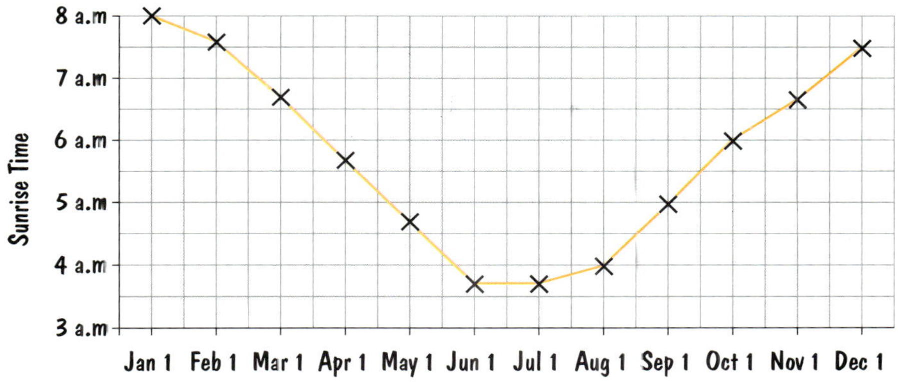

What happens to the sunrise times between January and June?

2. The table below gives the sunset times for the first day of every month over a period of 12 months.

MONTH	Jan 1	Feb 1	Mar 1	Apr 1	May 1	Jun 1	Jul 1	Aug 1	Sep 1	Oct 1	Nov 1	Dec 1
SUNSET TIMES(pm)	4	4.45	5.45	6.30	7.30	8	8.15	8	6.45	6	5	4

a) Draw a line graph to show the information in the table.

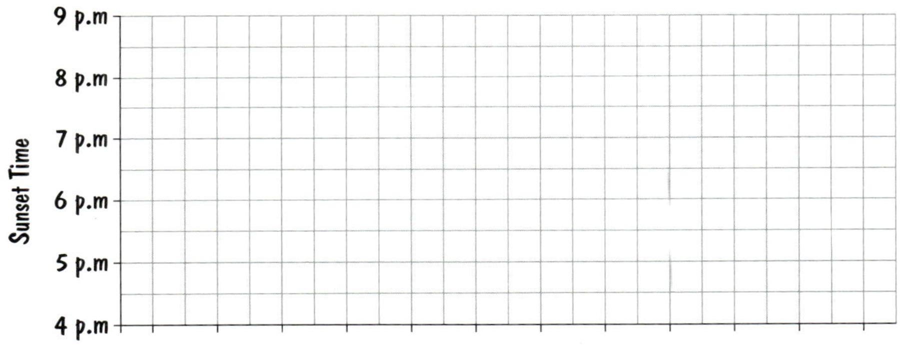

b) What pattern is there between the sunrise and sunset times over a period of 12 months?

3. Tom decides to measure the length of shadow formed by a tree in his garden at different times during the day.

TIME	9 a.m	10.30 a.m	12 noon	2 p.m	6p.m
Length of shadow formed	5m	4.5m	4m	4.6m	5.7m

a) How is the shadow of the tree formed?

b) Why is the shadow formed at 12 noon the shortest?

c) What would the length of the shadow approximately be at 4pm?

d) Why does the Sun appear to move across the sky during the day to produce the shadows of different length?

NOTES